HOW TO MAKE BRILLIANT STUFF THAT PEOPLE LOVE

HOW TO MAKE BRILLIANT STUFF THAT PEOPLE LOVE . . .

AND MAKE BIG MONEY OUT OF IT

Patrick W. Jordan

JOHN WILEY & SONS, LTD

Other Wiley Editorial Offices

John Wiley & Sons Inc., 111 River Street, Hoboken, NJ 07030, USA

Jossey-Bass, 989 Market Street, San Francisco, CA 94103-1741, USA

Wiley-VCH Verlag GmbH, Boschstr. 12, D-69469 Weinheim, Germany

John Wiley & Sons Australia Ltd, 33 Park Road, Milton, Queensland 4064, Australia

John Wiley & Sons (Asia) Pte Ltd, 2 Clementi Loop #02-01,
Jin Xing Distripark, Singapore 129809

John Wiley & Sons Canada Ltd, 22 Worcester Road,
Etobicoke, Ontario, Canada M9W 1L1

British Library Cataloguing in Publication Data

A catalogue record for this book is available from the British Library

ISBN 0-470-84711-5

Typeset in ITC Garamond 11/15pt by Footnote Graphics, Warminster, Wiltshire.
Printed and bound in Great Britain by Biddles Limited, Guildford and King's Lynn.
This book is printed on acid-free paper responsibly manufactured from sustainable
forestry in which at least two trees are planted for each one used for paper
production.

CONTENTS

ACKNOWLEDGEMENTS

Thanks to all at Carnegie-Mellon University Design School, where this book was written during my tenure as Nierenberg Professor of Design.

The ideas and insights in this book have been gathered over years of working in design and marketing. Thanks to my co-workers and clients past and present.

Thanks also to all those at Wiley who helped in the creation and production of this book, especially Claire Plimmer, Rachael Wilkie and Peter Hudson.

Finally, thanks to Jackie Jones for support and encouragement.

1

How to make brilliant stuff that people love and make big money out of it

Introduction

As its title suggests, this book is about how to make brilliant stuff that people love and make big money out of it. The approach outlined here is based on my experience as design and marketing consultant. I have used it with clients all over the world in a wide variety of industries. Traditional industries such as cars and electronics. Modern industries like the dot.coms and the telecoms. Medical and professional services. Fast-moving goods, fashion, financial services, domestic appliances, even charities. Clients in all these sectors have used this method and found it to be effective in providing customers with great products and services that they love. Of course my clients have loved these products and services too! They have been profitable and given a healthy boost to the bottom line.

Three Steps to Success

The approach outlined in this book isn't rocket science. It's really very simple. Just do three things – understand the consumer, know what they want, give it to them. Do those three things and you've got a pretty good chance of having a winning product on your hands. Yet the sad reality is that very few companies do these things. They don't realize they should be doing them, or they can't be bothered to do them, or they don't think they can afford them, or they don't know how to do them, or they don't have the skills to do them properly. Reading this book won't give you the skills to do them. But if you're in design or marketing or have some half-decent designers or marketers in your organization, then you've already got those skills. It is going to tell you why you need to use them and how to use them. It will explain how you can use the approach on any budget. Obviously the more you can spend the more thorough you can be, but you can still gain a huge advantage on even the smallest of budgets. Hopefully the motivation will come when the advantages become clear!

The start point is getting to know your customers. *Really* getting to know them – respecting them, putting yourself in their shoes. What's important to them? What motivates them? What are their hopes, fears, dreams, aspirations? How do the products and services that they buy and use reflect these aspirations? It's about providing pleasure to people through the stuff we create for them. Both through the design of the product and the way that the product is marketed. What does the product or service do for them? How do they feel when they are using it? How does it make them feel about themselves? Respect for the customer is a philosophy that underpins every aspect of this approach. It is not a quick fix for tricking people into buying tat. It is about establishing a bond between producer and customer. A mutually beneficial relationship with trust on both sides. Or, in market speak, sustainable competitive advantage through enhancing the quality of our customers' lives.

This book is about pleasure. What is it? How do we deliver it? We will start with a little bit of theory, delving into the worlds of anthropology and philosophy to build a simple framework for looking at what makes people feel great. We'll use this as a start point for understanding the kinds of questions that we need to be asking ourselves about our consumers. We'll look at how to create a persona – a fictitious person who acts as our customers' representative in the design process. The persona is the central figure in our quest to make great stuff. We need to keep focussed on this person, determined to understand their every need. Once we've done that we can get an understanding of the role that our product or service will play in their life and the kinds of benefits that it can deliver to them. The third and final step is to go make a product or service that delivers those benefits. We analyze the various elements that go into the design and marketing of stuff and see how we can use them to make a game plan for delivering the benefits that our customers want. A game plan that we can use to deliver a wonderful experience for our customers – products that are not only useful and usable, but also a genuine joy to own and use.

In Search of Pleasure

Since the beginning of time, humans have sought pleasure. We have gained pleasure from the natural environment.

From the beauty of flowers or the feeling of the sun on our skin. From bathing in soothing waters or the refreshment of a cool breeze. We have actively sought pleasure, creating activities and pastimes to stretch our mental and physical capabilities or to express our creative capabilities. Cave-dwellers wrestled to test their strength and expressed themselves through painting on the walls of their dwellings. Today we 'pump iron' in the gymnasium and decorate our homes with selections of paintings and posters.

Another source of pleasure has been the artifacts and services with which we have surrounded ourselves. For centuries humans have sought to create functional and decorative artifacts, which have increased the quality of life and brought pleasure to the owners and users. Originally, these objects would have been clumsily bashed out from stone, bronze or iron by unskilled people who simply wanted to make something for their own use. As systems of trade and barter were developed, specialist craftspeople became prevalent, creating artifacts for use by others in the community. Today, most of the artifacts that we surround ourselves with were created by industry. Services have seen a similar evolution from benefits exchanged within primitive communities to multinational on-line trading services.

Pleasure

What is pleasure? The *Oxford English Dictionary* defines it as 'the condition of consciousness or sensation induced by the enjoyment or anticipation of what is felt or viewed as good or desirable; enjoyment, delight, gratification. The opposite of pain.'

In the context of making brilliant stuff that people love, we can define pleasure as:

The emotional, hedonic and practical benefits associated with products and services.

Practical benefits are those that result from the outcomes of tasks for which the product of service is used. For example, in the context of a word-processing package, a practical benefit could be the effective and efficient production of neat, well-presented documents. Meanwhile a washing machine, for example, delivers the practical benefit of clean, fresh clothes.

Emotional benefits come from how stuff affects a person's mood. Using a product or service might be, for example, exciting, interesting, fun, satisfying or confidence-enhancing. A computer game, for example, might be exciting and fun to use, while a stylish new gown may give the wearer a feeling of self-confidence.

Hedonic benefits, meanwhile, refer to the sensory and aesthetic pleasures associated with products. For example, a person might recognize a product as an object of beauty or might enjoy the physical sensation of touching or holding a particular product. A well-designed chair may be physically comfortable to sit on and may also be an 'objet d'art' worthy of aesthetic appreciation. Meanwhile, a shaver might give pleasant tactile feedback, both in the hand and against the face.

In a sense, this definition is a 'catch all'. Indeed it is intended as such. In order to create brilliant stuff that people love it is important to start by considering *all* of the potential benefits that a product or service can deliver.

The Four Pleasures: A Framework for Considering Pleasure with Products

Given that pleasure with products is defined so broadly, it is useful to find a way of structuring our thoughts on the issue. Here we can look to the academic discipline of anthropology for some help. Anthropology is the study of human cultures and communities. One of the world's leading anthropologists is Professor Lionel Tiger from Rutgers University in New Jersey. He has spent much of his career studying pleasure and human motivation and has devised four categories, which between them span the different types of pleasure that humans can experience. Here they are. (You can read about them in more depth in Tiger's book, *The Pursuit of Pleasure*).

Physio-pleasure

Physio-pleasure is to do with the body and with pleasures derived from the sensory organs. They include pleasures connected with touch, taste and smell as well as feelings of sensual pleasure. In the context of products, physio-pleasure would cover, for example, tactile and olfactory properties. Tactile pleasures concern holding and touching a product during interaction. This might be relevant, for example, in the context of a telephone handset or a remote control. Olfactory pleasures concern the smell of the new product. For example, the smell inside a new car may be a factor that effects how pleasurable it is for the owner.

Socio-pleasure

This is the enjoyment derived from relationships with others. This might mean relationships with friends and loved ones, with colleagues or with like-minded people. However, it might also include a person's relationship with society as a whole – issues such as status and image may play a role here.

Product and services can facilitate social interaction in a number of ways. E-mail and mobile phones, for example, facilitate communication between people. Other products may facilitate social interaction by being talking points in themselves. For example, a special piece of jewelry may attract comment, as may an interesting household product, such as an unusually styled TV set. Indeed, mobile phones are also an example of a product whose styling is likely to influence people's perceptions of the owner. Association with other types of products may indicate belonging in a social group – Porsches for 'yuppies', Doc Marten's boots for skinheads. Here, the person's association with stuff forms part of their social identity.

Psycho-pleasure

Psycho-pleasure comes from people's mental and emotional reactions. In the case of products, this includes issues relating to the cognitive demands of using the product or service and the emotional reactions engendered through the experience of using it. For example, it might be expected that a word processor that facilitated quick and easy accomplishment of, say, formatting tasks would provide a higher level of psycho-pleasure than one with which the user was likely to make many errors. The former word processor should enable the user to complete the task more easily than they would with the latter. The outcome may also be more emotionally satisfying and less stressful.

Ideo-pleasure
Ideo-pleasure is about people's tastes, values and aspirations. On the most basic level, a taste might mean preferring one color over another or preferring a particular type of styling. Stuff that is aesthetically pleasing to the consumer can be a source of ideo-pleasure through appealing to the consumer's tastes. Values could be philosophical or religious or may relate to some particular issue such as the environment or a political movement. Such values can be embodied in stuff; for example, a product made from biodegradable materials might be seen as embodying the value of environmental responsibility.

Aspirations are about how people want to see themselves and what they hope to become – what we aspire to be like as people. Maybe career and financial success is a priority; perhaps the family comes first; perhaps being cool and trendy is important. Whatever our aspirations, the stuff that we own and use can be a source of pleasure through helping to affirm our self-image. For example, if we aspire to being sophisticated and having good taste, then maybe we can have this self-image reinforced through owning furniture that is tastefully and elegantly styled. Meanwhile if we like to think of ourselves as energetic and exciting we may have this self-image affirmed through driving a high-performance car.

In the context of making brilliant stuff that people love, the four pleasure framework is a useful tool for taking a structured approach to design and marketing. It is perhaps best to think of it as a practical tool and not to worry too much about exactly where the borders are between each of the four pleasures. From experience of using this approach I have found that the boundaries between each category can sometimes be a little fuzzy. But that doesn't matter. The key issue is that using the framework can help to make us more thorough and methodical in our approach than would be the case if we tried to approach the whole thing in an unstructured way.

Need Pleasures and Pleasures of Appreciation

Another helpful mentor in understanding the nature and meaning of pleasure is the Christian writer and philosopher C.S. Lewis. In his treatise *The Four Loves*, Lewis includes an essay on what he describes as likings and loves for the subhuman. Within this essay he considers natural entities, such as plants and animals, but he also looks at products and services. Lewis classifies the pleasures that can be derived from such entities as being either 'need pleasures' or 'pleasures of appreciation'.

Broadly, need pleasure can be seen as the pleasure that is gained from the removal or discomfort or some other kind of negative state. Drinking a glass of water would give a need pleasure to someone who was thirsty. Pleasures of appreciation, meanwhile, are those that are pleasurable in and of themselves. They are pleasurable even if we were perfectly contented in the first place. For example, a person might enjoy a fine wine for its taste and bouquet and for the pleasant feeling of intoxication that it delivers. They may have been perfectly happy and comfortable in the first place, but will feel even more so when they are drinking the wine. On the other hand, it seems unlikely that someone would wish to drink a glass of water unless they were already thirsty.

The key insight that we can gain from Lewis's approach is that products can be pleasurable either because they help to facilitate positively joyful feelings and experiences or because they help us to eliminate negative situations or feelings. When making brilliant stuff that people love, we should bear both of these things in mind.

2

Understanding people

Understand People Holistically

The start point for making brilliant stuff that people love is to understand the consumer. Understanding the consumer is not just about gathering market research data or defining the demographic or socio-economic category of the target consumer group. Rather we need to develop an empathy for those for whom we are making stuff. We need to understand them as people, not merely as a set of statistics. My experience has been that the most effective way of approaching the consumer is to create a persona – a made-up person who is representative of the consumers who you are serving. That is not to say that the statistics aren't important. Indeed the clearer we are about our target consumer group and the more we find out about that group the more chance we have of creating a persona who will represent the target group well in the design process. Nevertheless, whether we have the stats or not, it is very helpful to 'humanize' the target consumer group through creating a character who embodies the target group's characteristics.

As an example to illustrate how to create personas and how to use them in the design process, imagine that we were designing a photo camera. Imagine that market research has identified an opportunity to sell cameras to young women who, the research suggests, are under-served in this market.

The company decides that it will create a product aimed at Western women aged between 25 and 35 of high socio-economic status. Our task is to come up with a camera design and a marketing campaign that will connect with this group and meet their needs. We will develop this example as a case study throughout the book as a means of illustrating the various stages of creating pleasurable products.

The first stage in the design process is to create a persona to represent the target group. This person may be someone who we feel represents the average of the group or it may be someone who represents an extreme, either because this extreme is aspirational or because it raises particular issues that need to be addressed. In the case of this group, for example, a 25-year-old woman who had become a million-aire through running her own on-line travel business might be someone who would be aspirational for the group, even though – or perhaps because – they would represent an extreme of the target group.

The use of 'extreme' personas has proved particularly powerful when addressing issues of universality in design. Universal design, or 'inclusive' design as it is known in Europe, refers to the creation of products that can be used by disabled people and non-disabled people alike. While the average person in the target group may not be disabled, there may be merit in creating a persona with a disability in order to address certain issues in the design process. If we design something so that a disabled person can use it then the chances are, in respect to the issues affected by the disability, that it will also be OK for non-disabled people. The TV remote control is a great example of a product that was originally designed for disabled people, but that has proved popular with everyone. Good Grips® kitchen tools were originally designed for people with arthritis but, because they are so easy to handle, have also proved extremely popular with professional chefs.

This same principle applies with other issues too. In the case of attitudes towards products and services, for example, some in a target group may tend to take a more skeptical attitude towards stuff than others. Some kinds of stuff seem to attract skepticism. Stuff to do with losing weight or making us healthy, for example, or products and services that are claimed to be environmentally responsible. If we're making those kinds of claims then we can be pretty sure that there'll be people questioning them. Quite right too. If we're going to make claims we're going to have to back them up. The idea of using a skeptical persona is that if we can design something that will convince the skeptic, then we can be fairly confident that our design will also be convincing to less skeptical people.

Returning to our example, let's go for a persona who is not necessarily extreme, but still somewhat up-scale socio-economically of the midpoint in the target group. This can help to give a good balance between some of the practical issues that we will need to consider and the potential for creating something that will be aspirational for the con-sumer. Practical considerations would include, for example, usage scenarios and marketing issues, such as pricing and channels to market. By choosing a persona who is at the higher end of the target group in terms of socio-economic status and lifestyle, we can create a product that fits a lifestyle that those in the target group will aspire to and that is more or less in reach. This gives added value to the product through creating a link between it and a desirable way of life.

Case Study Part 1 – Leigh Francis

Let's call our imaginary persona Leigh Francis. Leigh is 28 years old, a freelance fashion journalist living in the trendy Tribeca neighborhood of New York in-between the fashionable SoHo and Chelsea districts. Although she has achieved a lot already she is very ambitious and wants to keep climbing the career ladder, perhaps getting an editorial job on one of the nationals or a fashion magazine. She is prepared to put in long hours because she believes that hard work is the key to success.

Nevertheless, work is not her whole life; she is a keen sports player – an active member of the local tennis club. She enjoys tennis matches, not only for the fun of the game, but also because she knows that it helps to keep her fit, providing a good balance to the sedentary nature of her job. She also enjoys the social aspect of the tennis club, especially a drink and a chat with her girlfriends in the club bar.

Leigh is dating Mark, a 35-year-old stockbroker who lives in his own apartment in the West Village, another up-scale, though somewhat more traditional district. She is very fond of Mark and they have a lot in common – they are both ambitious people and love the trappings of a yuppie lifestyle. They spend most weekends alternating between each other's apartments. They enjoy sampling the fine cuisine of New York's upscale restaurants, going to contemporary art exhibitions and watching Broadway shows.

Leigh keeps in regular contact with her parents, phoning them at least twice a week. She loves to tell them all about her work and the wonderful lifestyle she leads. They are very proud of what she's achieved – they had always wanted her to have the opportunities in life that they had never had. Her parents live in a quiet rural village in Missouri in the mid-West. Leigh still has many friends there. She sees them a couple of times a year when she goes home to visit her parents. Her friends are slightly in awe of her glamorous lifestyle. Leigh knows this and takes a secret pleasure in it – she is proud of what she has achieved so far and knows she can be even more successful in the future.

3

Understand what people want

Product Benefits

Having created a persona to represent our target consumer group, the next stage would be to go through each of the four pleasures in turn and to understand what the persona might want from a product. We will return to Leigh throughout the book as we develop this case study further. But for now let's return to the four pleasures framework and delve a little deeper. We'll look at each of the four pleasures one by one. Each section is packed full of examples of the kinds of benefits that people might want from stuff, and of great products and services that have succeeded in the marketplace through delivering them. There are also hints for how to understand and predict how people react to products and how to leverage design and marketing techniques to increase sales and revenue.

Physio-pleasure

At the most basic level, a product should physically fit the person for whom it is designed. Consider, for example, the layout of a vehicle interior. The driver is seated behind the wheel and from that position has not only to drive the car, but also to operate a number of in-car controls. These will include, for example, controls to operate the in-car stereo, controls for the air conditioning, controls to change the speed and gear ratio of the engine and the turn signal controls. If the driver cannot easily reach all of these controls then they will experience difficulties, which are likely to have consequences that range from annoying to threatening. Not being able to adjust the air conditioning, for example, might result in discomfort, whereas having attention diverted from the road while trying to get an awkwardly placed control could have potentially fatal consequences.

Many other products also have to accommodate people's body dimensions. These include medical products such as x-ray machines and scanners, personal care products, such as sunbeds and, perhaps most obviously of all, chairs and seats. Many people in the Western world spend the majority of their waking hours seated. People sit in their workplaces, sit in their cars, sit at home to eat and watch TV, sit in bars, cinemas, sports arenas, theatres, etc. Two basic requirements associated with seating are that seats should be comfortable and that the person sitting should not be physically damaged by the seat.

Comfort has proved a surprisingly difficult thing to meas-ure as it is something that people often don't notice. They notice when they are feeling some discomfort though, which has traditionally led designers to define operationally com-fort as being an absence of discomfort – in the terms of C.S. Lewis, it has been operationalized as a need pleasure as opposed to a pleasure of appreciation. The basic design rule for creating comfortable seating seems to be to make seating as adjustable as possible. Aspects such as the height of the seat from the floor, the angle of the backrest, the height of the arms – all these should be adjustable. People come in all different shapes and sizes and seats should be adaptable to this.

One of the most imaginative approaches to creating comfortable seating was that taken by Norwegian designer Peter Opsvik who, more than 30 years ago, created the Balans Variable Seat. This design, which most people thought looked kind of quirky when it first came out, has the user perching upright on the seat while featuring a knee-rest to kneel on. This design gives a more even spread of weight across the body rather than concentrating it all at the base of the spine. This is a great example of a designer helping to create a great product through challenging the stereotypes of the day – 'thinking out of the box', to use the business vernacular. When people thought of chairs they thought of products with four legs, a seat and a backrest. Opsvik broke through this stereotype to create a design that has remained popular and commercially successful to this day. Not so quirky now!

Another category of products where getting the physical dimensions right is critical is portable products. The size of the product is likely to affect how easy it is to move around, but the weight is likely to be even more crucial still. Strength can vary widely between different people – products that are portable for one person are not necessarily portable for another. This seems a very straightforward issue, yet it also seems to be one that is often overlooked. For example, many TVs that are sold as 'portables' would be far too heavy for many of the elderly to carry – the weight of these products is, then, excluding many of the potential user group from receiving the benefits of portability. Sometimes there may be an element of danger associated with portable products. For example, kettles have to be moved from one place to another when full of boiling water – dropping a kettle full of scalding water could be very dangerous.

Some portable products are moved across surfaces rather than actually lifted and carried by the user. Many vacuum cleaners are examples of this. Here, then, the issue will be not so much how heavy the product is, but how maneuverable it is. Most vacuum cleaners are fitted with wheels and are pulled or pushed by the user. It is important that these products can be maneuvered without being bumped against other household objects as this may damage the product and, probably more importantly, the object against which it is bumped. One way of making vacuum cleaners more maneuverable is to put a swivel wheel at the front. This makes the product much more responsive to the user's control and has been used as a selling feature for a number of vacuum cleaners.

Hand-operated products are another potential source of user discomfort. In the 1950s, Finnish designer Olaf Backstrom made a study of scissors design. He noted, for example, that scissors were often designed in such a way that those using them for long periods of time – for example, tailors, designers and artists – could end up with painful calluses and blisters on their hands. In response to this, he created the O-Series range of scissors for Fiskars in 1960. These scissors had a long rectangular handle that users gripped from the outside, plus one finger hole, which enabled the user to keep their hand firmly located in place. This contrasted with traditional scissors designs, which encourage the user to stuff a number of fingers into each finger hole, creating pressure points between the user's fingers and the edge of the handle – this can lead to blistering.

Similarly Zdenek Korvar, a Czech sculptor and designer, carried out extensive work on the ergonomics of hand tools at around the same time. He was interested in understanding the causes of cuts and blisters on factory workers' hands. He set up user trials with workers using existing tools (hammers, pneumatic drills, etc.). Korvar wrapped a soft plaster sheath around the outside of the products before giving them to the workers to use. After use he looked at the imprints made by the workers' hands. He used this as the basis for designing grips that fitted the hand snugly when the products were in use.

Korvar's approach of modeling the product grip to the users' hands has been reflected in the design of many of the recent generations of Japanese hand-held video cameras. These have been designed so that they grip the user's hand firmly and snugly, enabling them to move the camera around as if it were almost an extension of the body. Indeed, sometimes the shapes of these devices give the feeling that they have evolved biologically rather than having been fabricated. They almost appear to have been implanted in the body to form an extension of the arm.

From great control in use, let's get back to our search for comfort. Clothing is a product area where comfort is a high, even paramount, consideration. Of course this wasn't always so. Going back to the turn of the twentieth century, there seemed to be a fashion for wearing clothes that would have been distinctly uncomfortable, but which were regarded as beauty-enhancing – the corset being the epitome of such a garment. In recent times, however, attitudes towards comfort have become very different. For example, in the late 1970s and early 1980s tracksuits and training shoes had become part of mainstream – 'high-street' – fashion, largely because they were such comfortable leisurewear. This style was later adopted by designers of high fashion – 'catwalk' fashion. Examples of the leisurewear influence on catwalk fashion can be seen in Michiko Hoshono's spring/summer collection from 1994 and, in the same year, Donna Karan's DKYN Diffusion Line, which incorporated elements of American sportswear.

If comfort is defined – at least operationally – as an absence of discomfort, then it is clear that products can offer physiological pleasures that go beyond comfort and into the realms of sensuality. In other words, products can provide the user with sensations that are physically pleasurable in and of themselves, even if the user felt perfectly comfortable in the first place. Continuing with the example of clothing, there are certain materials that feel particularly pleasant against the skin and that can provide a positive sensual experience to the wearer. A silk shirt feels great against the skin, for example.

Hand-held products can also be sensually pleasurable to the touch. This sensual experience is shaped not only by the form of the product but also by the properties of the materials used. A great example of products where this has been put into practice is the Norelco range of shavers (this product also retails under the name Philishave in Europe). This product is pleasurable to hold both because of its pleasing organic shape and because of the use of rubber-like silicon in combination with the matt plastic finish that forms the main part of the body. Philishave have highlighted the sensuous properties of the product in both their print and TV commercials and the company continues to dominate the electric shaver market worldwide.

In the case of the Norelco shaver, the sensual properties of the product add greatly to the pleasure in use. However, clumsily applying sensual materials without thinking properly about the context in which the product will be used can sometimes be more of a negative than a positive. For example Olivetti, inspired by a design movement of the time, experimented with rubber membrane keyboards on their products in the early 1970s. The experiment proved less than successful as although the keyboards may have felt superficially nice to touch they also felt stodgy and imprecise.

When considering what would be the most appropriate tactile feeling for any situation, the context of use should be considered paramount. Keyboards are for writing. People want precision, speed and good clear feedback when they press those keys. The Apple Macintosh keyboard feels great to use. It is light and nimble and the keys give a good reassuring click every time you press them.

Sometimes it is the result of using stuff that gives us physio-pleasure, rather than the stuff itself. For example, the taste of coffee produced by a coffee maker may be dependent on a number of design issues, such as the speed at which water drips through the filter and the temperature at which the coffee is kept after filtering. Indeed, many coffee makers now have adjustable brewing processes in order to offer the user a variety of tastes. This is a great example of how a product can offer extra features in order to enhance the outcome of the result and to give users more control and variety.

Another kind of physio-pleasure stuff can deliver to the consumer is olfactory pleasure. Perfumes and colognes, for example, can make the consumer smell pleasant and attractive. The design of scents is an area that is increasingly drawing on science to understand what smells elicit particular associations and emotional responses in us. Musk, for example, is something that people tend to associate with masculinity, while floral scents are perceived as being more feminine. Scent manufacturers tend to be among the most sophisticated in terms of understanding the link between the design of stuff and how stuff is marketed. One and BE by Calvin Klein, for example, are designed to have a gender-neutral, or gender-ambiguous, scent. This is reflected, for example, in the choice of fairly androgynous-looking models for the marketing commercials. It is also reflected in the design of the scent bottles, which have a form and coloring that is explicitly neither masculine nor feminine.

In contrast Giorgio Armani's Emporio Armani products are two separate scents which, although they have clear similarities, are nevertheless distinctly for men and women. They have achieved this through the use of a number of common ingredients, married with a number of ingredients that are distinct between the two. This 'similar yet different' theme is also reflected in the design of the cologne and perfume bottles, which are both cylindrical but with subtle differences in color and form. These bottles are also used as the focus of the TV commercials with the focus on their sensual design qualities. Both the Calvin Klein and the Armani offerings are great examples of how to take an integrated approach to design and marketing. The product, the packaging and the advertising all tell the same story, reinforcing the key product benefits.

Scents are products whose primary benefit lies in their olfactory properties. Sometimes, however, the olfactory properties of stuff can appear to be incidental and yet in reality have a significant bearing on how pleasurable the product is to own and use. People may associate particular smells with quality, for example. The 'new car smell' that you experience when sitting in a new automobile is an example of this. It's a smell that people associate with quality – so much so that it is now possible to buy cans of 'new car smell' air freshener to keep that feeling of quality in your car. This phenomenon has not been lost on used car dealers who, in addition to giving a used car a thorough clean and polish, will also often spray this air freshener inside the car before showing it to potential customers.

Another way in which stuff can be a source of physio-pleasure is through altering our state of physiological arousal. For instance, products can make us alert or make us relaxed. Products containing stimulants such as sugar and caffeine would be examples of the stuff that would increase alertness; meanwhile products that contain alcohol will tend to make us more relaxed. Again, this is often reflected in the marketing campaigns for these products. Soda manufacturers such as Coca-Cola and Pepsi, for example, tend to use upbeat, high-energy imagery in their campaigns. One of the most spectacular of these campaigns was one created for Pepsi Max, which used images of extreme sports such as base jumping (parachuting off cliffs and buildings), to give the drink an association with high-adrenaline excitement. The company has also created tie-ins through sponsoring extreme sports events and even through a Pepsi Max computer game that simulates extreme sports. Interestingly the campaign also helped to reposition this diet drink as something for men as well as women to enjoy.

Socio-pleasure

Socio-pleasures are to do with – in the broadest sense – our relationships with others. This includes personal relationships with friends, co-workers or loved ones and it also encompasses more abstract relationships with society as a whole. Examples of the latter include our social and economic status and our sense of belonging and social identity.

The last few years have seen a revolution in communications. E-mail and cell phones have become almost ubiquitous and the text-based short messaging service (SMS) is proving extremely popular with cell phone users in Europe and the Far East. It is surely only a matter of time before SMS also takes North America by storm.

Mobile phones provide a clear and distinct advantage over landline phones. When you make a call to a landline you are calling a location. If the person you want is in that location then fine, if not then you don't get to speak to them. There are also clear and obvious advantages to owning a mobile phone. You are far less likely to miss important calls. You can call people wherever you are, which is convenient sometimes, important other times and maybe even lifesaving on occasions. The ubiquity of the mobile phone has also created a new kind of social dynamic, particularly with respect to arranging social events.

Before mobile phones became so popular, people would tend to arrange their evenings out by calling a long time in advance and arranging a pre-agreed time and venue to meet.

Now people tend to call at the last minute and come to an agreement about the meeting time and place depending upon what is the most convenient at the time. This phenomenon is something that I have found particularly prevalent in London. While people may often agree in advance to go out on a particular evening they will rarely set the time and the venue until the last minute. Often it will be a case of ringing people and saying, 'Where are you now?' and then picking a venue that is mutually convenient to everyone – usually a bar near an underground (subway) station that is easy for everyone to get to.

The problem for those Londoners who do not have a cell phone is that there is a danger that they will get left out of the social loop or will force their friends to plan early entirely for their benefit. This is likely to make them at best a nuisance and at worst very lonely! While having a cell phone in London was once a luxury, it has now got to the point where it is more or less a social necessity. What was once a pleasure of appreciation has become a need pleasure. This phenomenon – known as the 'tipping point' – is common among devices that support social interaction. When a new product starts out, few people have it and it is a luxury. If the product proves popular then more and more people get one and then eventually a point is reached where people start to assume that everyone has one. This, of course, happened with fixed line telephones a long time ago; it has happened with e-mail in most societies and is the case with cell phones in the majority of the western industrialized world.

While the success of cell phones is easy to understand, the success of SMS is something that at first sight might seem somewhat baffling – I have to admit it initially baffled me! By any of the conventional rules of design, the service is pretty awful. Typing messages is cumbersome, fiddly and inelegant. The messages appear on a small screen, in small type that is difficult to read and they are delivered over networks that can be unreliable, especially at peak times, which by definition is most likely to be the time that people most want to send messages. It seems an obvious place for designers to step in and do a better job. Interestingly though, this may be a rare case where lack of usability actually brings benefits in terms of the social dynamics of the product.

Puzzled by the huge success of SMS, I commissioned a series of studies from a number of universities and a user research bureau. The studies looked at the ways in which people used different media to communicate. This included cell phones, fixed line phones, e-mail and SMS. A distinctive feature of communication using both e-mail and SMS as opposed to phones is that they are asynchronous. You get time to think about the other person's message and compose a reply within your own time. Many of the people we observed and spoke to in our study cited this as an attractive quality of e-mail and SMS, as they felt that it gave them time to think of something appropriate to say. In business correspondence they could think the issue through and come up with a carefully thought-out response. In personal correspondence they could take their time to create a message that would have the right emotional effect. If they wanted to say something witty then they could think of something witty to say. If they wanted to say something romantic, then they had time work out something really nice that would express how they felt. If they were feeling angry they had time to regain their composure before firing back a message.

While e-mail and SMS are both asynchronous, they differ hugely in terms of the volume of data that they can deal with. With e-mail it is only the size of the correspondents' servers or e-mail accounts that limit the amount of data that can be transferred. With a reasonably sized e-mail account there is almost no limit on the amount of text that it is possible to transfer. Even a free Internet e-mail account should be able to deal with an amount of text that would be equivalent to many hundred times the contents of Tolstoy's famous door-stop of a book, *War and Peace*! It is also possible to send and receive attached files containing documents, presentations or images.

SMS by contrast is extremely limited in terms of the amount of data that can be sent. The service is only able to handle a maximum of 160 characters, including all spaces and punctuation. Of course, in many situations this is a huge disadvantage. However, there is one very important social situation in which it is a blessing – when you want to make contact, but you don't really have anything to say. This is also where the difficulty in use becomes an advantage. Because the recipient of the message knows that you don't have much space to write in and that it takes a long time to type a message out, they are likely to be happier with a brief message than they would be if the message were delivered through another medium.

For example, if you received an SMS message from a loved one saying simply something like 'missing you' then you might feel quite pleased. You would know that it would have taken some time to type in and in any case there wouldn't be much room for a more involved message. On the other hand if you received an e-mail, eagerly opened it and saw only the words 'missing you' in the text then you might be disappointed. You might have expected at least to get some of the person's news and you would know that typing two words on e-mail is a pretty minimal effort. You might end up feeling that if the other person is unwilling to put any more effort than this into communicating with you then perhaps they don't care about you as much as you thought!

So while cell phones, e-mail and SMS have all proved to be big hits through facilitating communication, each has its own properties that give it a unique place in the market.

While communication devices facilitate social interaction in a fairly obvious way, there are many other types of product that have succeeded in facilitating social interaction in other ways. Clear examples would be transportation products such as automobiles, trains, ships and aircraft, which have helped to bring people together from across long distances and which have enabled people to experience societies and cultures geographically far removed from their homes. However, there are some products that have social implications in more subtle ways, perhaps through having a role in a social gathering or ritual or maybe because they are associated with some kind of social significance or meaning.

Perhaps one of the most effective marketing campaigns of all time was that launched by diamond company De Beers in the first half of the twentieth century. At the time the diamond industry, which was by this stage more or less completely owned by De Beers, was in difficulties. Because of a previous glut in the market, diamonds were not necessarily seen as the luxury stone of choice in a time when precious stones were primarily seen as a reflection of socio-economic status. De Beers succeeded in making diamonds fashionable again through creating an association between the stone and romantic love. Up until this point there was no commonly perceived connection. Diamonds looked great and were associated with wealth and high socio-economic status, but then again so were emeralds, sapphires and other fine gems. De Beers launched a well-coordinated campaign to promote diamonds as the stone of romance. Specifically, their marketing campaign of the time was aimed at persuading people that the diamond ring was the only serious token of engagement.

Among other promotional approaches, the company ran advertisements in women's magazines. These depicted scenes of men proposing to their sweethearts and offering diamond rings to seal the engagement. Now familiar messages accompanied the advertisements. Slogans such as 'A diamond is forever' became part of the language, the implication being that if the love was everlasting it should be sealed with a gift that is everlasting. Women were also encouraged to see the giving of a diamond ring as the only true sign that their lover was serious about them. The expression, 'If you ain't got the ring it don't mean a thing' was born. Indeed De Beers representatives even went into high schools to instruct teenagers in the etiquette of romantic love.

The campaign became so successful that it became almost a moral obligation for men to buy diamond rings for their fiancées. The implication was that if a man was not willing to buy a ring for his fiancée then he could not be serious or sincere in his love. Many of the early adverts in women's magazines also included a pull-out section that was aimed at men. This showed a chart illustrating the different sizes of diamonds and the comparative cost of each. The implicit question underlying it all was 'How much is your love worth'? Over the years 'guidelines' have been developed, such as the idea that men should spend a month's salary on an engagement ring. The diamond is an object that, through intelligent, if arguably cynical, use of marketing has become imbued with meaning and has come to represent love – the most priceless commodity of all!

Earlier we looked at mobile phones as great facilitators of communication. However, they also seem to be develop-ing a secondary social role as *the* contemporary token of social status. Before we develop this further, it is worth making a distinction between two broad kinds of social status. These are socio-economic status and cultural status. Socio-economic status is something which can be established through shows of wealth, while cultural status tends to be achieved through shows of good taste.

Because mobile phones come in all shapes, sizes, styles and price tags they provide an ideal vehicle for people to express their social status. The study I commissioned into the use of communication devices showed that men in particular like to show off their phones. Walk into a bar in any European city and you will see men with their phones in front of them at the table. Phones seem to have taken the place of cars as the primary public indicator of social status for men. If you have a really cool phone you want others to see it. And the great advantage that phones have over cars in this respect is that you can't drive your car into the bar!

However, it would be wrong to give the impression that showing off mobile phones is purely a guy thing. Women also like showing off their phones, whether as status symbol or fashion accessory. Having a chic phone is becoming increasingly important to people and as it does so aesthetic redesign is becoming the major driver in the industry. Handset manufacturers are continually updating their offers – bringing an array of interesting and exciting designs onto the market. One of the most innovative approaches to handset design was Nokia's decision to come up with phones with removable panels. This allows people to change the appearance of the phone without having to replace the whole phone.

This design innovation proved a great marketing move on two levels. In the first instance consumers recognized the benefits of being able to change their phone's appearance without having to buy a new phone, giving this phone a clear benefit over the competition. Second, Nokia created a lucrative secondary market in the sales of the panels themselves. Once phones were on the market they were able to bring out new style panels on a regular basis. This secondary market can be particularly lucrative, as it means that even after the sale the handset becomes an ongoing source of revenue for Nokia. It also means that Nokia are selling directly to the public, whereas the majority of handset sales are to network providers who then sell the phones onto the public or give them away for free with the network contract. This means that it is usually the network operators who have direct access to the consumer. They will tend to buy mobile phones in bulk and squeeze the handset manufacturers' margins in order to maximize their own. Also, it is the network operators who are making the ongoing revenue from the sale of the handset as it is they who are profiting from the use of the phone. Through the sale of the panels, Nokia have created the same advantages that the network operators enjoy. They have a direct interface with the customer with no third party to squeeze their profits and they have also created an ongoing revenue source from the sale of the phone. A great example of how to leverage the sale of accessories in a fashion-driven market.

Now Nokia have spotted another great opportunity; in this case addressing the idea of the cell phone as the ultimate status symbol. They have set up a company called Vertu, which makes top-of-the-market mobile phones. And in this case 'top of the market' means way above anything else the market has ever seen before. These phones retail at up to $20 000 each and include luxury materials such as silver, gold and platinum. The faces of the phones are made from sapphire. The elegant styling and weighty price tag makes these phones top of the range with respect to both socio-economic and cultural status.

While cell phones may be the new kings of the status world, most products will have the capacity to convey status in one form or the other. Designing products that convey socio-economic status is largely about making it clear to anyone who is looking that the product costs a lot of money. In the yuppie era of the 1980s perhaps the ultimate status symbol was the Porsche sports car. This vehicle became synonymous with the young successful executive, working in financial institutions and taking home a huge salary. Owning a Porsche made an implicit statement: 'I'm young, I'm rich, I'm successful.'

While there is no suggestion that owning a Porsche is a sign of 'vulgarity', those who openly flaunted their wealth during this big boom in the city were often looked down on by others. It was felt by some that they flaunted their wealth in a vulgar and crass manner. In his television show during this period, British comedian Harry Enfield satirized the yuppie culture through a character called 'Loadsamoney'. This character, adorned in chunky gold chains, rings and bracelets, would tell everyone he met how rich he was and would always be carrying a substantial wad of banknotes with him. Whenever he went into a shop he would 'whop his wad on the counter' before making a purchase, even if it was just a newspaper or a packet of cigarettes.

Characters such as Loadsamoney are obviously exaggerated caricatures. Nevertheless, they are a great illustration of the difference between material status and cultural status. As well as his chunky jewelry, he is probably the sort of person who would enjoy 'flashy' products – stereos with hundreds of flashing lights, designer label clothes mixed and matched in a random, tasteless sort of way. He might wear the best Nike sports shoes with an Amarni suit. He would drink expensive German lagers straight from the bottle so that his fellow drinkers could see that he was drinking an exclusive brand, and he would eat in expensive foreign restaurants whose menus he would not be able to understand.

While Harry Enfield was parodying high-material status, low-cultural status people through Loadsamoney, disc jockey Steve Wright created a character 'Malcolm from the Arts Council'. Malcolm was the opposite of Loadsamoney. He was a parody of someone with high cultural status, but comparatively low material status. Malcolm would like designs that weren't flashy but that were 'profound'. Designs where he 'knew what the designer was trying to say'. His house would probably contain old, cheap junk – which

Malcolm would refer to as 'interesting period pieces' – rather than the latest offering from the Milanese studios. He would drink vinegar-like cheap wine, probably from some lesser-known Bulgarian vineyard, which he would describe as 'having a challenging palate'. Of course, Malcolm is as much an exaggerated stereotype as Loadsamoney. They are made-up comedy figures, but at least they help to make the point that products can confer status in different ways.

A subtle marketing variation on the theme of cultural status is the 'ironic' campaign, which puts a 'knowing' spin on something that might otherwise be seen as lacking subtlety and therefore perhaps cultural status. A good example of this is a campaign run by MG-Rover for the MG Z series. The adverts for the car were pretty much full-on 'guys' ads'. Lots of talk about power, adrenaline, speed, driving, acceleration. Towards the end of the TV commercial the guy doing the voice-over, who we are also led to believe is the owner of the car, starts talking about the interior of the car. He mentions its wonderful styling and its luxuriant seating and trim, which is made from the finest leather. In the very last line comes the knowing aside to the viewer. 'Well . . . at least it's not fur!'

The advert is fun and hedonistic and appears to be very much aimed at 'boys who like toys'. The last line is funny and makes what has come before somewhat self-parodying. The message that comes across is: 'This is a really cool car that kicks butt and I know I shouldn't really be so shallow as to like a car like that, but it's really neat and it's not *that* irresponsible, so what the hell.' Without the knowing aside at the end, the commercial would give the impression of a car for boy racers. But with the aside, it becomes a car for really smart guys who have a sense of humor and irony and enjoy playing at being boy racers, just for fun, when they get the chance every now and again.

So far in this section, we've mainly looked at products and services that have succeeded through making socially good things happen. However, products can also succeed through stopping socially bad things from happening – social need pleasure. Two major issues here are stopping vandalism and theft. A number of products are designed to discourage their own theft, while other products are designed to prevent the theft of something else. Car stereos, for example, are an example of a product whose design has evolved over the years both to minimize the chance of its own theft and to minimize potential damage to the car.

By the mid-1980s car-stereo theft had become a very prevalent crime, to the extent that people started to question whether it was even worth having a car stereo. Not only was it possible that the stereo would get stolen, but there was the added problem of the car itself being vandalized during the theft. Typically thieves would smash the glass in the driver or front passenger door in order to be able to gain access to the vehicle.

Over the years, designers have taken a number of different approaches to solving this problem. One solution was to make the stereo inoperable without the user first entering an alphanumeric code. As long as the thief didn't get hold of the code then the stereo was worthless to them. The problem with this approach was that from outside the car it was difficult to tell that the stereo was code-protected. It was only after having forced their way into the vehicle and removed the stereo that the thieves realized that they had been wasting their time. Unfortunately, this was of little consolation to the car owner who was left without a stereo and with a vandalized vehicle.

A far better solution is the car stereo with the removable front panel. In this solution, the controls to the stereo and some essential electrical connections are placed on a single removable panel. On leaving the car, the driver removes this panel, which fits easily into a handbag or a coat pocket. When a potential thief looks through the window into the car, it is immediately obvious that there is no point in stealing the stereo as it is useless without its controls. The driver gets to keep the stereo and the vehicle does not get vandalized.

Another socio-need-pleasure-inspired design and marketing opportunity is in creating products that help people to avoid social stigma of one kind or another. A great example of this is the Novopen™, a device for injecting insulin for use by people with diabetes. As its name suggests, the Novopen is designed to look like a pen and can be clipped into a jacket or trouser pocket. The pen-like appearance of this product contrasts sharply with that of a syringe. Syringes can have negative social connotations. First, their medical associations may emphasize the person's condition, something that they may not necessarily want to communicate to others. Second, their association with intravenous narcotic use is something that can be stigmatizing. By drawing on the metaphor of a pen, the Novopen plays down the medical nature of the person's condition and avoids all narcotic associations.

Psycho-pleasure

Psycho-pleasure is to do with how we feel when we use products and about the mental demands that using a particular product puts on us. The basic premise here is that stuff should be easy and fun to use. One of the key issues here is usability – Is the product or service designed so that people can get to do what they want to with it without having to work *too* hard or get *too* frustrated doing it? Of course, what is *too* hard or *too* frustrating will vary in the context of the product and what you are doing with it. Nevertheless, it is clear that some products are more usable than others and, generally speaking, the more usable the better.

Apple are perhaps the most famous example of a company who have built a brand on the basis of offering products that score high on usability. Indeed, when Apple first released their Macintosh computer it completely changed the face of personal computing. The Apple Macintosh was the first widely available computer to come with an interface where you used a mouse to point at stuff on the screen and then clicked when you wanted it to execute a command.

Before this operating a computer had meant typing in commands in the form of alphanumeric strings. This was cumbersome and meant that you had to either remember lots of different command names or that you had to have them written somewhere at hand. Furthermore these command line interfaces tended to be unforgiving of errors. One piece of punctuation gone awry would baffle the computer, suspending it in inactivity except for the return of a meaningless and unhelpful message, such as 'syntax error'.

The Apple Macintosh opened up personal computing to a whole set of people for whom computers might otherwise have been sources of fear and apprehension. In part this was indeed because the Macintosh made fewer demands on the user's memory for commands and because it was so forgiving of errors. However, it was also because there was something friendly about the way the computer looked. The graphics on the screen looked cheerful and familiar – files, folders, trash cans. The adverts for the computer were also lighthearted and fun, ranging from people doing fun creative stuff through to what could have been outtakes from America's Funniest Animals!

The whole Apple Macintosh image became one of fun and creativity. Through great design and effective marketing, Apple were able to change people's perceptions of what computers were. Rather than seeing them as being frightening, high-tech machines, unforgiving of error, people came to see them as helpful tools for getting stuff done and for self-expression.

While using computers may generate fear in some of us, there are loads of tasks that generate boredom and frustration. Right up there at the top for many of us are domestic chores, such as cleaning the house, doing the washing up and, worst of all, doing the ironing. For most of us, ironing is one of those chores that we just want to be done with as quickly as possible. This being the case, it is hardly surprising that the biggest selling point for an iron is its perceived speed. A number of my clients within the consumer electronics industry manufacture irons and their market research tells the same story over and over again. When it comes to how people make purchase choices, speed always comes out as the number one factor.

Companies are working to make irons faster. Chemical engineers are developing compounds which, when applied to the surface, will help to make the iron glide more quickly and smoothly over the clothes. Mechanical engineers are working on ways to finish the surface of the iron, reducing friction and so adding speed. There is also ongoing research into materials that heat up and cool down really fast, reducing the time you need to wait before the iron makes it to the right temperature for the type of fabric you are ironing. All this is great stuff and will undoubtedly make a positive difference to ironing speed. However, when researchers looked at how people judged the speed of an iron, one answer kept coming back – shape.

Irons that are sharply pointed at the front and that are lower in terms of overall product height tend to be perceived as faster. Strange as it may seem, it appears that people tend to project a speed metaphor onto irons that is derived from sea-going vessels. In this metaphor, the front of the iron represents the keel. The sharper the keel, the faster a boat will move through the water; the sharper the point of the iron, the faster the iron will move across the clothes. The lower a boat, the less wind resistance it will meet as it moves along; the lower the iron, the less the resistance to its movement. In other words, the closer the shape of an iron to the shape of a speedboat, the faster people perceive it as being.

Of course this is just a metaphor that we are sub-consciously applying. In rational terms it is a pretty lousy metaphor too. The iron doesn't cut through the fabric in the way that a boat cuts though water ... at least we would certainly hope not! And unless you're Superman you're not going to be moving the iron at the kinds of speeds where wind resistance is going to have any affect on ironing speed! Nevertheless, if you are in the business of making irons it is a metaphor you ignore at your peril.

Another domestic chore that is almost universally disliked is vacuum cleaning. Like ironing, it is something that most of us want to do well but to be done with as quickly as possible. Manufacturers have tried a number of innovations to help improve the speed and cleaning performance of vacuum cleaners – swiveling wheels that make the cleaner more maneuverable, attachments that can get into the most dif-ficult corners, easy-to-change dust bags, no dust bags at all.

Like irons though, there is a single feature that people consistently rate as the single most important indicator of speed. In this case it is the suction power of the engine.

While the speedboat metaphor for the irons had no basis in the reality of performance, the suction power of the vacuum cleaner engines does have a real relationship to performance. However, the relationship is not as straightforward as it might first appear. Up to a point increasing the power of the engine does improve speed and cleaning performance. The additional suction power means more dirt can be removed from the floor more quickly. However, at a certain point too much suction power can become a drawback as eventually the suction reaches a level where the cleaner hose more or less gets stuck to the floor. If the engine wattage gets ramped up too much the cleaner eventually becomes slow and difficult to maneuver. The result is a decrease in both speed and performance.

However, given that power is such a big issue in the eyes of the consumer, it can be beneficial to give the impression of great power, both in the design of the product and in the way that it is marketed. Many manufacturers draw on vehicle metaphors in order to bring across the power of their products. In particular, sledge vacuum cleaners – the ones that you drag along the floor behind the hose – are often shaped similarly to cars. Sometimes designers will put strategically placed bulges in the housing, giving the impression that the engine is so powerful that it is almost bursting, hot-rod style, out of the casing.

Ironically, consumers often judge a vacuum cleaner's power by the amount of noise it makes. The irony is that for years manufacturers have worked at minimizing the noise level, only to find that when they succeed at doing this, people start to lose faith in the performance of their product. One company tackled this issue head on in a TV advertising campaign in which they staged a series of 'power battles' between their vacuum cleaner and the machines of their competitors. The battles involved placing a ping-pong ball between the nozzles of two competing machines and switching the machines on. The winner was the machine that managed to suck the ball towards it and hold it firmly in place on the end of the nozzle. The manufacturers managed to show that although their machine was noticeably quieter than its competitors, it was also more powerful. Another of my clients took a different approach, simply deciding to do away with the silencing technology that they had taken so many years to perfect. The result was a cheaper and noisier cleaner, which proved a great success in the market.

In this case, customers were using the sound of the product as a means of judging its performance. Market research consistently shows that consumers use sound as a means of judging many aspects of a product's quality. In many cases the sound that a product makes will form part of the first impression that people gain of a product. People will usually 'hear' the product, or at least some aspect of it, before they actually use it. They will turn the vacuum cleaner on and hear the engine before they start doing any cleaning. They will open the drawer of their CD player and hear it click into place before they play any music. They will open the can of beer and hear the hiss as the ring-pull goes back before they take a drink. Just as with meeting new people, first impressions of a product count big. A good first impression and people are well-disposed to the product right from the off. But get it wrong and you've got an uphill battle to get the customer back on side.

Heineken, the world's biggest beer exporter, understand a thing or two about the importance of first impressions. The company has put a lot of time and a lot of dollars into getting the sound that the beer makes when you open the can just right. They carried out extensive research in order to find out the kind of 'hiss' that people associate with high-quality beer. They used this as a basis for designing the cans in such a way that, provided the beer is stored within certain temperature parameters, people will be greeted with this sound the second that ring-pull goes back.

Another industry in which the importance of first impressions is well understood is the motor industry. In this case manufacturers have focussed on the psychology of first impressions in the buying process. Typically when people are thinking seriously about buying a new car, they will want to take a look at it up close and then, if they still feel positive, eventually go for a test drive. However, before this, as the customer starts to get serious, one of the first things that they will do is to sit in the driver's seat, put their hands on the steering wheel and imagine driving it. Let's go through the process of getting in the car, action by action. It goes something like this. Grab outside door handle, open door, sit in car, grab internal door handle, close door, put hands on steering wheel, gear stick, etc. There are likely to be variations from case to case. For example, sometimes the dealer might open the door for us. But by and large we are likely to go through at least some of these actions when we first sit in a new car.

Because of this, the feedback that we get from these actions is very important in the selling process. Auto manufacturers are paying increasing attention to this. BMW for example, have put a huge amount of effort into getting the sound and feel of their closing doors just right so that it gives a reassuring, high-quality impression to the potential customer. It's important that when the doors close they do so with a good solid clunk. Any tinny sounds or, even worse, rattling noises and you've an uphill battle to make a sale. Fiat have carried out extensive research on the tactile properties of the handles and controls within the driver's reach; for example, the inside door handle, the gear stick and the steering wheel. Mazda and a number of other Japanese firms have analyzed how the aesthetics of the steering wheel affect people's first impression of the car.

As well as the period before any sale, the time period just after buying a new product can also be important psychologically. During this period, particularly if the product is an expensive purchase, people may want to feel reassured that they have made the correct purchase choice. Indeed, people will try to find evidence to reassure themselves. A survey by the advertising industry revealed that people are far more likely to look at advertisements for their new car after they have bought it than before they make a purchase. This phenomenon is known to psychologists as 'cognitive dissonance'. Basically, it translates as 'the search for evidence that confirms what you already want to believe'. If we have just spent several thousand dollars on a new car, then naturally we want to believe that we have made a good choice and spent the money wisely.

This early period of ownership is also going to be formative in terms of how people think of a product. It is probably the time period in which they will be paying most attention to the product. They will want to feel excited with what they have and good about themselves for having bought it. In the case of advertising material for vehicles, the sort of material that is effective for after-sales reassurance may be different from what is needed to attract a customer's attention before the sale is made. A great example of this is the material that Subaru used to advertise their Impreza WRX range, a car that attracted huge press acclaim as soon as it hit the showrooms in 2001. In addition to a series of TV commercials and glossy brochures, which brought across the excitement of driving the vehicle, the company also collected a series of press cuttings about the car and compiled them into another brochure. These articles contained journalists' opinions of the car and many also went into deep technical detail about how the car had performed during test drives.

While the press cuttings and performance data is interesting, reading through the brochure containing all that stuff would be a pretty heavy time investment. It is difficult to imagine many people being prepared to read that much detail about a car as part of the purchase decision. After all, they may have several alternative choices in mind and it would not be realistic for many of us to find the time to study them all in such depth. However, where this brochure really scores big is with people who have already bought the car. This gives them a host of information about it, which they can browse through at their leisure. All of it is positive and reinforcing, underlining the wisdom of the decision they have made. There is a saying in the motor trade: 'It's not about selling someone one car, it's about selling them three or four cars over 15 years.' If you want that repeat trade you've got to impress your customers and keep on impressing them right up until the point when they are ready to buy a new model. Reinforcing the wisdom of their decision to buy from you is a good start.

When you buy a new car you get to use it straight away. As soon as the dealer has signed it over to you, you get to drive it away from the forecourt. For many products this is not the case and consumers have to go through an installation sequence before they can get the product up and running. This installation sequence is the manufacturers' chance to screw up big time in the eyes of the customer. Often the customer will return home with their new stereo, TV, computer or whatever it is they have bought and two hours later will be frustrated, annoyed and all round ticked off with the product, themselves, the retailer and the manu-facturer. This has traditionally been the time of misery in between the excitement of the purchase and, hopefully, the joy of use.

Sorting out a spaghetti-like jumble of wires in order to connect up the components of a stereo, searching forever to try to load in all the different channels on the TV tuner, working through endless commands, manuals and licensing agreements to get all the software installed on a computer – by the time the product is ready to use, the customer may have lost all enthusiasm for it. They may be cursing them-selves for ever having bought it in the first place and be angry with the manufacturer and the retailer for having made them go through such an agony in order to get the thing working. What's worse, they may not have installed it properly, mean-ing that the product will function sub-optimally through its whole life cycle. Failing to wire up all the speakers properly, missing a couple of channels out or installing them in a different order to how they are listed in the TV guide, leaving some extensions out of a software installation – all of these things will lead to sub-optimal service from the product and keep the user from gaining the full benefit of it.

Companies are getting increasingly wise to the importance of the installation stage. Many TVs now come with auto-installation of channels. Stereos often have clearly labeled or color-coded wiring plans and retailers will usually install much of the computer software you need in the store. One of my clients, a company in the consumer electronics business, aims to design their TVs so that it takes 10 minutes or less from the time that the consumer removes the TV from its packaging to when it is fully operational. They test their designs with consumers and won't accept the final design until this criterion is met. It's a smart move on their part. Customers maintain the excitement from the moment they make the purchase. The ease of installation underlines the correctness of the purchase choice that they have made. Ease of installation was also a major consideration in the design of Apple's i-mac computer. This comes with all the software pre-installed. All the user has to do is 'plug and play'.

Another source of psycho-pleasure is enjoyable mental challenges or puzzles. A product type where mental challenge and emotional enjoyment are right at the top of the agenda is computer games. Computer games have become a multibillion dollar business. Specialist games consoles such as the PlayStation and the X-Box have sold in vast quantities all over the world. Meanwhile a steady stream of games for the PC continue to be a commercial success, bringing pleasure to many millions of people worldwide. Games can bring pleasure through the puzzles and challenges that they set for us. Some games can be an emotional roller-coaster, bringing us excitement, triumph, tension and disappointment in equal measure.

Well-designed games should engage us. In other words they should take us into the world of the game. In our minds we should be the warrior, the sports star or the bounty hunter, not a person sitting in front of a screen moving pixilated shapes with a control pad. The concept of engagement was originally identified by Aristotle when he was analyzing what made good drama. He noted that one of the tenets of good drama is that the audience should be immersed in the world of the play. That instead of sitting in the theatre thinking, 'I'm watching some actors acting out a script', they should be thinking, 'The bad guy has just murdered the emperor', or whatever the story happens to be. Again, the marketing campaigns associated with games have a big role to play here. X-Box and PlayStation, for example, run a number of their TV adverts in the style of movie trailers, helping people to get to know the characters and the basics of the plots and scenarios.

The aesthetics of a product can also have an effect on the level and nature of psychological arousal on the user. One design element known to have an effect on arousal is color. For example, the combination of yellow and black is one that we are hardwired to be wary of. Animals that sting, such as bees and wasps, have this color combination. Even some insects that don't sting have also adopted it just to make themselves look more dangerous. The color combination protects them by warning off other animals. When they see those colors on an insect, animals 'think' to themselves, 'Uh oh ... those guys can sting.' Designers have drawn on this phenomenon in order to warn people away from products that are dangerous. Warning signs are often colored yellow and black as this raises our alertness and attracts our attention to the possible danger.

Just as yellow and black seem to be associated with danger, so red seems to get the pulse racing, making us feel stimulated and energetic. Perhaps this is the reason that it is often favored by manufacturers of performance cars, Ferrari being a notable example. Red also seems to say, 'Use this in an emergency.' Fire extinguishers are red, as are most emergency shut-off buttons. Green by contrast means, 'Go!', whether it be a traffic light or an on-switch. Whether this is genetically or culturally mediated is debatable. Nevertheless it seems to be more or less a worldwide convention, which manufacturers of safety critical equipment would be foolish to ignore.

Blue and green tend to be colors that make us feel more relaxed. A possible explanation for this is that they are colors that we are drawn to in nature. Blue has associations with water and clear skies, while green is associated with lush vegetation. When our cave-dwelling ancestors were in a well-vegetated area, under a clear sky near a clean supply of water, then everything was fine. They felt relaxed and, so the argument goes, we feel calm in the presence of those colors today. These colors can be used to good effect in situations where we wish to encourage people to be calm. It makes sense, for example, to use them in situations where people might be nervous – a dentist's waiting room or the interior of an airplane, for example. We wouldn't want to use too much red if we were trying to keep people calm. Italian movie director Michelangelo Antonioni once got his production crew to paint the canteen red in an effort to get his actors psyched for the tense scenes in a movie that he was shooting. It worked – kind of. The record doesn't show how it affected the actors, but within a week fights were breaking out in the canteen between other staff on the movie set. He had it repainted!

As well as being associated with calm, blue is also associated with trust. This is probably one of the reasons why it is a color that is often favored by banks and other financial institutions where trust and reliability is the name of the game. It is difficult to know whether this is a biological or an environmental thing. Off hand there doesn't seem to be any obvious biological reason why we should feel that blue is something that we can trust. Nevertheless, the association does seem to work all over the world. One of the major Korean banks, for example, carried out a study in which they looked at how people responded to certain colors on the screens of ATM machines. The aim was to find a color that would enhance the users' feelings of trust, both in the bank and in the ATM itself. Again, blue came out as the color most associated with trust.

Ideo-pleasure

Ideo-pleasure relates to people's tastes, values and aspirations. Tastes are about our personal judgements about what we like. They are judgements which are about preference but without any explicit component of moral judgement. For example, I may think that blue clothes look better on me than red clothes. Given the choice of buying a blue sweater or a red sweater I would, all things being equal, choose the blue sweater. That is not to say, however, that I believe wearing blue sweaters is in any way morally preferable to wearing red sweaters.

Value judgements, by contrast, are preferences with a moral component to them. For example, if a person were concerned with the environment they might regard it as a moral responsibility to buy only environmentally friendly products. Aspirations, meanwhile, are about how people wish to define themselves. A person might aspire to be a good parent, a modern man, a traditional woman, a career woman, a good husband. All these are possible ways in which people may define themselves. Their choices with respect to the stuff that they own and use can help to reinforce these self-images or may undermine them.

By their very nature, tastes are likely to be the least stable of these, because they are not based on judgements of moral value or desired self-image. They may change fairly rapidly. That is not to say that they definitely will. Some people may be very consistent in their preferences. Nevertheless, the constant streaming onto the market of products with new aesthetics is testimony to how people's tastes change. Many industries are largely based on catering to the need for aesthetic novelty. The fashion industry is probably the most obvious example. However, it is not the only one. Many consumer electronics companies continually repackage old technology inside new aesthetics. Car companies will bring out new variants on old themes that mechanically are more or less indistinguishable. Indeed, people getting bored with things and replacing them even when they are still performing fine functionally is, arguably, vital to the economy. If people stopped getting bored with stuff and stopped throwing it out and replacing it with new stuff, there is the possibility that the economy would grind to a halt!

Tastes are difficult to predict with any degree of sureness over anything longer than the very short term. Even then many 'predictions' may rely on a fair degree of hegemony in order to be fulfilled. Consider, for example, the fashion industry. Predictions tend to be a season at a time. 'Next season lace will be in.' 'Belts are the new must-have fashion accessory.' 'Red is the new black.' Even though I have been working with clients in the fashion industry for a number of years, I have to admit that I am still at something of a loss as to how these things are really decided. Suffice to say it is a somewhat nebulous process involving having one eye on what the 'cool' people on the street are wearing and one eye on what the leading fashion designers have chosen to foist on an unsuspecting public!

Often a consensus will develop in the industry. By this I mean the industry in the widest sense, not just the fashion houses, but also those who analyze fashion, such as trend forecasters and fashion journalists. In the end the predictions are likely to become self-fulfilling. Imagine, for example, that a top fashion house decides that red is the color for the new season. Journalists are tipped off. The fashion magazines tell everyone that red is the color for the new season and show lots of glamorous models wearing nice red clothes. Other fashion houses think to themselves, 'Better go with red this season.' People look at the magazine images and start to like red clothes, even if they may not have been to their taste before. Red clothes become popular and sell well. Everyone is happy. The customers have some nice new clothes. They feel good and the whole industry is telling them, as one, that they have made the right decision. The fashion houses are happy. They have had another successful line, which has been profitable and received critical acclaim. The forecasters are happy because their professional judgement has been vindicated. The journalists are happy. By getting it right yet again, they have demonstrated that they have their fingers on the pulse!

Recently companies have started employing new techniques both in order to improve the accuracy of their predictions and to increase the power of their hegemony. A manifestation of the former is the rise of the 'coolhunter'. Coolhunters are people whose job it is to seek out the coolest people, look at what they are wearing and use this information in order to advise designers about the sorts of things that will be the 'next cool thing' in the mass market. The idea behind this is that while most of us like to be cool to one degree or another, there are a few mega-cool people out there who are way ahead of the coolness game. What is cool to them now is what we will all find cool in a few months' or years' time depending on the industry. In more traditional marketing theory terms, these mega-cool people are the innovators – the first people to start using a particular product. The next wave of people are the early adopters. Early adopters are very cool people, but not quite as cool as the innovators. They will be among the first people to catch onto what the innovators are doing and, if they like it, they'll get the same stuff. Next come the early majority, still pretty cool people. For a mass-market smash hit it is important to get to the early majority. This is what makes the difference between a mass-market product and a niche one, and it is not always easy to do. Marketers call it 'crossing the chasm'.

In many industries, production techniques are advanced and cheap enough to enable manufacturers to make a profit out of comparatively small runs of products, so it is not *always* necessary for a product to cross the chasm in order for it to be worthwhile. Coolhunters seek out both trends that they expect to be niche as well as possible mass-market trends. Selecting the coolest people is a somewhat subjective issue. However, there are certain places where, according at least to coolhunter wisdom, the coolest people tend to hang out. While more and more manufacturing companies are employing coolhunters, the sectors that tend to make most use of them tend to be clothing and sneaker manufacturers. Levi's and Puma are among the better publicly documented examples.

At the time of writing, the coolest place in the world is probably Brixton in London. It certainly is if coolness is measured in terms of the density of the coolhunting population! Coolhunters gather in packs opposite Brixton underground station, watching the unsuspecting passengers as they emerge into Brixton Road. Mental or written notes are made. What are the coolest people wearing, what do their sneakers look like, what have they been reading on the tube? Sometimes there are photos and even interviews with the coolest-looking people. Where are they going out? What is their favorite music? What movies have they been to see? What products have they bought recently? Observations are e-mailed to clients all over the world and within a matter of months products start appearing on high-street shelves with an aesthetic that has been influenced by what has been learned from the coolhunters' observations. Sooner or later the places that are currently the coolest will become less cool. The coolhunters move on and the process will start over again.

As viral marketing techniques become more and more sophisticated, coolhunters also have a role to play in increasing a company's hegemony within the marketplace. Viral marketing techniques are about getting business through 'accelerated' word of mouth. Like coolhunting, this relies very much on a bottom-up view of marketing. Viral marketing techniques speed the word-of-mouth process using a number of catalysts. Technology is one of these. People can be encouraged to send their friends messages by e-mail singing the praises of a product, or to contribute to websites disseminating information about the product. A good example of this is the Amazon.com books website. People are encouraged to write reviews about any books that they have read and these are then posted on the website so that those visiting the site can see their views.

Coolhunters have become involved in a form of viral marketing that involves distributing products free to really cool people in the hope that this will help them to catch on with others. They will often seek out the coolest kid in the neighborhood and give them the latest pair of sneakers to wear. The hope is that when other kids see that the cool guy is wearing the sneakers, then they will want a pair like that too. This kind of approach has also been tried in the workplace and even in schools. Recently Hasbro, a company specializing in the marketing of computer games, launched a viral marketing campaign based on distributing products to kids they termed 'Alpha Pups'. Alpha Pups are the kids in school that others admire and look up to because they think they are cool. Again the idea is that when the other kids see the Alpha Pups using the games they will also want to play them as it has become a cool thing to do.

This form of viral marketing is appealing to people on an aspirational level. It is based on the idea that 'I could be more like that really cool person if I had what they have or did what they do'. Products become aspirational when they have a meaning in our minds that would make us feel positive about ourselves if we owned or used them. People may attach meaning to products because of the design of the product, the way the product is marketed, because of who else is using the product or because of the product's history.

A great example of a product that has acquired its meaning largely through its history is the Harley-Davidson motorcycle. These motorcycles became associated with a nonconformist, rebel image through their association with the Hell's Angels. This was not an association that was encouraged by Harley-Davidson. Indeed, in the early days of the Hell's Angels, the company refused to supply parts to shops known to service Hell's Angels' motorbikes. Nevertheless, in the long run it is arguably an association from which the company has greatly benefited, not only in terms of sales to the Hell's Angels themselves, but also because it has helped to create a legend around the product. The brand has developed a meaning that is so strong that people even have the logo tattooed on their bodies. There can't be many other products that inspire that kind of devotion. Some people have even got married by swearing oaths on the Harley maintenance manual ... for goodness sake!

In parallel to their rebel image, Harley-Davidson products have also developed something of an all-American image. Again, this was something that was not necessarily deliberately developed by the company, but rather something that originally arose out of a combination of circumstances, the first of which was the US Army's decision to use Harley-Davidsons as troop motorbikes during the Second World War. Later, when the US motorcycle market became flooded with imports in the 1970s and 1980s, many saw Harley-Davidson as the lone US company, struggling against this 'foreign invasion' of their markets – again strengthening the all-American image. The patriotic associations with the motorcycle are part of what gives it such a wide appeal. We can enjoy the rebellious image without being seen as un-American in any way.

While the Harley's image may have developed through accidents of history, the company is now building on its heritage in its current marketing campaigns. Recently they ran a series of commercials on TV showing an old man telling stories to his grand-kids. He tells them of how he dreamed of getting a Harley and riding across the States, having all kinds of adventures. The kids look on wide-eyed with interest and ask him to tell them more. He then admits that he never got around to buying the Harley, but instead did the 'sensible' thing and invested the money in aluminum shares. At this point the kids lose interest and run off to go see Grandma. The message is clear. A Harley-Davidson isn't a cycle for sensible people. It's for exciting, fun people who want to have adventures. People who aren't afraid to rebel. People who live their dreams.

Harley-Davidson have experienced a dramatic upturn in commercial fortunes in recent years. If you bought shares in Harley a few years back, then you're laughing all the way to the bank right now. It seems that Harley-Davidsons are now finding favor among the middle-aged, professional classes. People who may have seen themselves as being rebellious when they were younger, may now feel frustrated by the apparent mundanity of their lives. Owning a Harley-Davidson can be an outlet for the rebellious side of their nature. After a hard week working as an accountant or a solicitor, people may enjoy getting on their Harley and speeding through the countryside. Not only can this be exhilarating in itself, but it can also reinforce a more exciting, less conformist self-image.

Another vehicle that seems to have 'accidentally' become associated with a country – in this case the UK – is the Mini. This car was launched in the UK in response to the Suez crisis of 1956. The idea was that a small car would be more efficient in terms of fuel consumption – an important financial consideration at a time when oil prices were very high. In the event, by the time the Austin Mini came to the market in 1959, Britain was heading for the boom times of the 1960s. Austerity was the last thing on the consumer's mind as the country entered arguably the most optimistic decade in its history. On the face of it, the Mini appeared doomed to failure. Aside from fuel economy, the car didn't score high on any of the measures that would normally be looked at as a mark of quality in a vehicle. It was small, it didn't go very fast, it wasn't luxurious.

Despite this, the Mini went on to be one of the most successful British cars of all time. Indeed, it became an icon of Britain in the 1960s. Ironically, the 'sensible', fuel-efficient, economy car became a symbol of urban chic, driven by rock stars, the young and the beautiful. It was almost a 'star' in its own right. The Kings Road in London was full of Minis during the 1960s and the car was even featured in films such as *The Italian Job*. A significant contributor

to the Mini's success was the car's association with Britain —
even this was somewhat ironic as the car was designed by
Alec Issigonis who is Turkish – in a decade in which Britain
was making a huge impact on popular culture. This was the
time of 'Youthquake' – a loose 'movement' of creative young
people such as the Beatles, the Rolling Stones and Mary
Quant. These people transformed the international music
and fashion scenes and did so in a way that put a great deal
of emphasis on the value of youth. In the 1950s the best thing
to be was to be rich. In the 1960s the best thing to be was
young.

The Mini was strongly associated with youth. It became
the young person's car of the decade. This may have been
in part due to its styling, which was very different from
anything else on the market at the time and which had
something of a 'fun' feel to it. However, the low cost of the
car almost certainly played a role here too. The Mini was
one of the lowest-priced cars available on the market and
at the time this made it affordable for younger people of
all social classes. Young, working-class people may have
started work at the age of 16 and, in the booming economic
climate of the time, would soon have been able to afford to
buy a Mini.

Meanwhile, the children of wealthy families may have
been able to persuade their parents to buy the car for them.
As the Mini became associated with youth, and as youth
became so highly prized, older people, desiring the youthful associations, also started buying the car, eventually

making it one of the best-selling cars of all time. If you wanted to feel young, you bought a mini. Recently BMW, who now own the rights to the Mini brand, relaunched the car, restyled for the new century. Once again though, the marketing campaigns emphasize the fun image associated with the car, bringing a great brand back to life with the sporty Mini Cooper.

Other products appear to develop particular lifestyle associations through their functional properties. An example of such a product is the Zippo cigarette lighter. These products are designed so that they give a very strong and powerful flame, which will not blow out even in the windiest of conditions. This functional quality makes the lighter ideal for any sort of outdoor use and has led to the association of the product with a broad series of lifestyles. One such lifestyle is that of the all-American great-outdoors man – the type of lifestyle embodied in the Marlboro cigarette advertisements. However, the Zippo lighter has also become something of a symbol of the hippie culture – associated with the camper van and music festival scene. Here the stereotype is of people sitting out on the grass, smoking and chilling out. The Zippo, then, has built up a broad constituency of customers, based on one particularly strong, functional benefit – the ability to work outdoors in windy conditions.

The examples we have looked at so far have emphasized products that are aspirational because of their cool, exciting, rebellious or youthful associations. However, there are any number of reasons why a product may be aspirational for a person. It all depends on how people want to see themselves.

Social and lifestyle trends can provide clues to the sorts of aspirational qualities that people may look for in products. A major trend at the moment is the changing roles of men and women. As men's gender roles become more and more fuzzy, manufacturers are spotting opportunities to sell products across stereotyped gender boundaries. For example, men are increasingly becoming involved in domestic tasks and childcare. While many men will enjoy these roles, they may still feel a little uncomfortable about using products that they may see as having traditionally feminine associations. A number of companies have seen commercial opportunities here and have come up with childcare and domestic products with overtly masculine styling.

One result of the changing roles of men and women is that men are increasingly to be seen pushing their kids around in strollers. In parallel with this there has been a booming market in strollers with 'masculine' aesthetics. These often have three large wheels, come in a black and chromium color scheme and borrow a number of aesthetic elements from sports vehicles. Kids are strapped into the seat in a manner that would not be out of place on the racetrack! These 'sport' strollers have been a huge hit with men and have come to dominate the stroller market. Not only do they look manly, they also have some pretty manly names! Examples of such products include the Urban Detour

Glacier from Mothercare and the Techno Stroller from Maclaren.

We've looked at tastes and aspirations. The third aspect of ideo-pleasure relates to how products can appeal to or offend people's moral values. A major issue here is the effect of products on the environment. Care for the environment has become a major issue over the last few years and most of us will be reluctant to use or purchase products that are environmentally irresponsible. Oil and gasoline companies in particular have become particularly sensitive to charges of environmental irresponsibility and many are making concerted efforts to improve both their performance and image in this area. A glance at the Shell website, for example, will reveal news about the progress of various environmental projects that the company is involved with.

They have also developed an environmental theme in their TV commercials. In one of these a young woman talks about her passion for the environment, and how she is working hard to protect its natural beauty. At first the viewer might suppose this is a promotional message from an environmental protest group. The woman then reveals she is an employee of Shell Oil. BP are another oil company who have caught on to the importance of having an environmentally friendly image and have redesigned their logo to give a sunny, natural look.

Other companies have developed ethical associations through their philanthropic work. One area that is receiving particular attention is education. In the UK, for example,

Walkers, the potato chip manufacturer, have implemented a program called 'Books for Schools'. This program allows schools to trade in tokens that kids have collected for school books. Coca-Cola have a similar program, 'Reading is Fundamental'. Coke aim to donate in-classroom libraries to over 10 000 underprivileged communities. Oil company Texaco are another who sponsor education through their philanthropy. Their philanthropic policies mean that when you buy something from them you are indirectly contributing to the educational programs that they support.

Products may acquire their 'moral' properties through the way they are marketed or the philanthropy of their manufacturers. However, the moral products may also be embodied in the product itself. For example, people may object to a product if the labor conditions of those who made it are unfavorable. Nike, for example, have been boycotted by a number of people who feel that they subjected workers in Vietnam to poor working conditions. The boycott has been highly organized with a number of professional-looking websites and many who feel strongly on this issue may have been dissuaded from buying Nike products. Products may have been made in a way that is good or bad for the environment. The Honda Insight, for example, is the first mass-market gasoline-electric hybrid on the market. Great on fuel consumption, this car is likely to appeal to those for who the environment is a major concern.

Sometimes people may regard certain types of product as being immoral in and of themselves. For example, some people feel that tobacco products and alcoholic beverages are immoral. In cases like these manufacturers are often left in a dilemma as to whether to defend their product or simply to try to ignore the criticism and hope that the debate will fade away. Of course, if you are going to fight back, you had better have some ammunition to back up your claims! The alcoholic beverages industry, for example, tends to keep a close eye on what emerges from medical research into effects of alcohol. From time to time, medical studies appear that find alcohol-related health benefits. For example, it is suggested that moderate amounts of alcohol may protect people from high blood pressure and heart disease. Industry bodies such as the Wine Institute help to disseminate information that can help to enhance the view of the industry's products in general.

Case Study Part 2 – Product Benefits

We have looked at the four pleasures, examples of how they can be delivered through good design and marketing and at some great techniques and concepts for investigating what people want out of a product. Now let's return to our case study and see how these can be applied to creating a photo camera for our target group of young women of high socio-economic status. We'll look at each of the four pleasures in turn and see how we can use them to come up with a specification of the benefits that this product should deliver to our target group. When we do this we'll look through the eyes of our persona, Leigh Francis, in order to work out what it is that she would want in a camera.

Physio-pleasure

A camera is a hand-held device. Leigh, like anyone else, is going to prefer a camera that feels great to hold and radiates a feeling of quality every time she picks it up.

Product benefit: Camera should feel good in the hand.

Leigh is going to be using the camera when she's out and about. She's not a professional photographer who's going to want a camera that sits fixed on a tripod in a studio. It's got to be easy to carry around.

Product benefit: Camera should be easy to carry around.

When taking a photograph, she's going to hold the camera to her face and look through the viewfinder. The camera is going to come into contact with parts of the face, in particular the side of the nose and the eyebrow. The camera should fit neatly and comfortably to her face.

Product benefit: Fits well and comfortably against the face.

Leigh likes to take care of her nails. She doesn't want these broken or damaged when she's using the camera. No fiddly or high-resistance little buttons or catches.

Product benefit: Camera should be operable without causing damage to the user's fingernails.

Socio-pleasure

Leigh is going to be using the camera in public places, which means that others are going to see her using it. She's a successful woman of high socio-economic status. The camera should get this across. A kind of badge saying, 'I'm a successful person.'

Product benefit: Camera should confer the impression of high socio-economic status on the user.

Leigh's not just a 'Loadsamoney'. She's got great taste too. Let's reflect this by throwing some cultural status into the mix.

Product benefit: Camera should confer the impression of high cultural status on the user.

Leigh's going to be taking photos of her friends. Unlike professional models, they are going to get pretty ticked off if they have to stand around posing for ages while Leigh tries to get the perfect photo. The camera's got to allow her to take photos quickly. Anyway, Leigh doesn't want to have to mess around trying to set up a shot. The fun moments that she wants to capture will be gone before she's captured them. Make it quick!

Product benefit: Camera should enable the user to take photos quickly.

Leigh enjoys cultural activities. Trips to the gallery, the opera. She enjoys nice restaurants. She wants to take photos without disturbing others or drawing too much attention to herself.

Product benefit: Camera should be operable without disturbing others or embarrassing user.

Psycho-pleasure
It's not the process of taking the photos that Leigh enjoys, but the outcome. She wants great quality snaps and she wants them fast. They don't have to be professional quality, just nice shots that she can enjoy. This reinforces the speed point that we mentioned above. Let's add in good quality photos as a new benefit.

Product benefit: Camera should enable the user to take good quality photos.

We hope Leigh's going to love the camera, but we can't expect her to spend ages reading though the manual, working out how to use it. She should be able to take it out of the box and get going with it straight away.

Product benefit: Camera should be easy to use at the first attempt.

Ideo-pleasure

The camera should look great. Leigh's going to be carrying it around with her and she's going to be looking at it every time she takes it out. Make it look great so that she can enjoy it every time she sees it.

Product benefit: Camera should look great.

Leigh's a modern woman and she wants a camera that reflects that. Don't give her something that looks like it's a toy for the boys. She wants something tasteful and feminine.

Product benefit: Camera should reflect the user's femininity.

Like many people of her generation, Leigh is environmentally aware. She's not going to be happy about buying a product that's bad for the environment.

Product benefit: Camera should be environmentally 'safe'.

By considering each of the four pleasures in turn and applying Leigh's persona in the context of each, we've got a set of benefits that define what would make a great product for the group of consumers she represents. If we can deliver these we'll have a great product

that will meet the wishes and demands of our target group.

In the next section we'll look at a way of structuring the delivery of product benefits through design and marketing. Then we'll come back to the case study and see how we can use this structure to create a camera that our target group are going to love.

4

Delivering what people want

Properties of Products and Services

When we looked in depth at the four pleasures, we saw how stuff could deliver various types of pleasure to those who own or use it. Perhaps it was the aesthetics associated with a product or service that made it pleasurable, maybe it was the functionality. Sometimes a product was pleasurable because of how it was to use. Sometimes the narrative of the marketing campaign was what people loved. Usually, people loved stuff for a combination of reasons – a number of elements coming together to make a great overall experience. In the sections ahead we'll take a look at the elements that go to make up the design and marketing campaign. These can be thought of as the building blocks that we can use in order to construct a great experience for the user. There are lots of them, so we'll zip though each one quickly. I'll bring back some examples from the four pleasures section in order to illustrate them as well as throwing some new examples into the mix.

Functionality

What the product does and how well it does it. You can sit on Opsvik's chair and be super comfortable. You can use most cell phones to call and send text; some allow you to send e-mail. Games do things to entertain you. Air filters get rid of impurities and keep you well. Some products are loaded up with virtually every feature but the kitchen sink. Loadsamoney might like those, as they allow him to show off to his friends! Sales people also tend to like them as they can reel off a list of features to potential customers. Too much functionality can get in the way of usability. Having to wade through a stack of buttons to find the functions you need can be irritating and many manufacturers are now moving away from over-featured products.

Color

Blue for a boy, pink for a girl. Black is classy. Blue is trust-worthy. White is pure. These are some of the associations that people tend to make. At least we do in the West. In some countries in the Far East, for example, people associate white with death. Color is a great way of invoking associations with a product. Ferrari make all their cars red (unless requested otherwise). Red is fiery, exciting, powerful, passionate, fast. All the things that Ferrari aim to be. Red has become part of the Ferrari brand just as trustworthy blue has for IBM. Because colors often evoke strong associations, appropriate use of color can be a great way of adding meaning to a design. But beware those cultural differences!

Form

Irons that look like speedboats look as though they go faster. Vacuum cleaners with bulging housings look more power-ful. Scissors that are shaped to fit the hand will be more comfortable. The form of the product can help deliver benefits to the user either through literally bringing benefits, as in the case of the scissors, or through association, as in the case of the iron and the vacuum cleaner. Arguably, in the case of the iron and the vacuum cleaner the forms are being a little deceptive, promising something that they don't deliver. The strollers with the big wheels and the 'roll bars' on the baby seat . . . Are they really more macho than any other stroller? Maybe not in function, but certainly in form. The rugged form gives a manly aesthetic and plenty of ideo-pleasure to many young fathers!

Product graphics

Friendly on-screen graphics were part of what made the Apple Macintosh such a user-friendly hit when it stormed cheerfully onto our desktops back in the late 1980s. Usually manufacturers can't resist the urge to stamp their logo on everything they make! The theme and the styling of the logo are likely to affect the way that people see not only the product, but also the company as a whole. BMW have a perfect circle, split into four perfect quadrants – precision engineering. Lucky Goldstar have something that looks like a cross between a symbol for an electrical component and a smiley face winking at you – they know what they're doing but they've got a sense of humor. There are a number of practical things to consider here too. Make sure controls and displays are clearly labeled. Make sure font is readable from where it is being read. What about the visually impaired? Will they need to be able to see the graphics in order to use the device properly? Does there need to be tactile instruction on the product through raised symbols or Braille?

Materials

Materials play a large part in defining the tactile properties of a product. The silicon grip on the Norelco shaver, the leather trim on the Rolls-Royce gearshift, the firm grip of the rubber on the handle of a high-end golf club. The materials used are going to be a major factor in the weight of the product. In the West, we tend to associate high quality with products that are heavy and thin. In the Far East people tend to prefer their products light. The materials used may have a major impact on how environmentally friendly a product is. Biodegradable plastics are better for the environment than standard ones. Some materials are more expensive than others. If you're making calls on a platinum cell phone, it's pretty clear that you're a person of high socio-economic status.

Sound

The sound of the BMW car door closing. The hiss as the Heineken ring-pull goes back. These sounds indicate quality. The roar of the vacuum cleaner engine indicates power. Mazda are another company who have paid a lot of attention to the sound their product makes. When designing the MX5 they wanted to recreate some of the magic of the British sports cars of the early 1970s, part of which was that throaty roar in the exhaust. They analyzed the sound frequencies and reproduced it. Just one part of what makes the MX5 such a highly acclaimed driving experience. We seem to associate deep sounds with quality. Apple give us a big booming bass tone when we power up the computer. Very reassuring. Sometimes the meaning associated with sounds can serve a very practical purpose. Shrill, loud sounds denote an emergency. Their sheer unpleasantness also makes us want to get out of wherever we are when we hear them. Sound can be an alternative means of communication with the visually impaired. The sonic beeps that denote that it is safe to use a crosswalk, for example.

Interaction design

Interaction design is about the mechanics of how people interact with a product. Products should be designed so that they are intuitive and easy to use. Put a push plate on a door that needs to be pushed and a handle on a door that needs to be pulled. Make it so that doing the obvious thing to do is also the right thing to do. That big red button on the side of the machine should be the emergency power-out, not the turbo-boost! Put the essential buttons such as volume and channel change in the most prominent position on a TV remote control. Give people a mouse to point at stuff on the screen rather than making them learn string after string of typed-in commands. SMS is one of those rare examples when 'bad' interaction design contributes to the social qualities of the product.

Packaging

Packaging serves a number of purposes, from keeping the product safe in transport, to conveying the product's benefits, to getting the product noticed on the shelf. The message sent out by the packaging should complement the qualities of the product. If a key feature of the product is environmental friendliness then it would not be very wise to package it in a non-biodegradable plastic box! Similarly, luxury packaging goes well with luxury products. Norelco came up with a great idea for their top-of-the-range electric shavers, selling them in specially designed pouches rather than the traditional cardboard box. Visuals and text on the package should be suitable in terms of the image they convey. If you are selling a domestic appliance aimed at the new man, then put a new-mannish-looking guy on the box! If you are selling a product that has significant health benefits or performance benefits, such as an energy drink or an air cleaning system, then spell out the benefits in the text. Want to get the product noticed on the store shelf? Big slabs of color tend to work best. Especially red. Of course this needs to be weighed with the pros and cons of a particular color in terms of the image of the product it conveys.

The Story

The marketing story is central to the campaign and the way that people perceive the product. De Beers created love stories for their print ads, with the diamond becoming the star at the moment the romance got serious! MG's TV commercials were about a guy rediscovering his enthusiasm for the hedonistic aspects of driving. These stories say something about the types of people who buy diamonds and MG cars. In the case of the former that they are romantic and caring, in the case of the latter that they are modern people, but they still know how to have fun The vacuum cleaner commercials told a story about how their product beat the competition in a suction power challenge. Here the story is being used to bring across a functional benefit.

Marketing Channels and Sponsorship

Marketing channels are where you show your advertisements for the product or service, be they print ads, TV commercials or any other medium. If you are going to run a TV commercial, the programs that it appears between are going to reflect perceptions of the product as well as, of course, whether the ad reaches the right target audience. If you're looking for an all-American image for your product and you've got the dollars to spend, then buying an ad slot at the Super Bowl is probably a good move. If you are looking for suave, sophisticated associations for your product then buying a slot at the Timber Sports World Championships probably isn't! It is if you make great outdoor products, though. Stihl, the power-saw company, realize this and sponsor the event heavily. Pepsi's sponsorship of extreme sports championships and the use of these events to promote Pepsi Max is a great example of how to make a great tie-in between a high-energy drink and a high-energy, exciting event. Coke and Walkers show social responsibility through their reading support programs.

Product Champions

Product champions are celebrities who are associated with the product through a marketing campaign. Generally speaking the image of the celebrity should be more or less in line with the image that you are trying to create for the product. For example, if you want the product to be associated with stalwart American values, then perhaps Clint Eastwood is your man. Looking for a sophisticated, elegant image? How about Cindy Crawford? Want to go totally left-field? Maybe you need to call Ozzy Osbourne's agent! Nike used celebrity sponsorships as a major tool in building their brand. In order to build an image of rebellion and victory, they sponsored a series of endorsements from high-profile rebellious and successful sports stars. John McEnroe was the first big star, controversial French soccer player Eric Cantona one of the latest. More recent Nike sponsorships have shown a desire to keep the success and competition side of the image going, but tone down the rebellion a bit. Michael Jordan has been their big star in this respect. Sometimes product champions can bring a touch of humor to an otherwise drab product. Lemmy, lead singer of heavy metal rockers Motorhead, advertising life insurance policies in a series of TV commercials that aired in the UK is a great example. Among the most successful celebrity endorsements have been Michael Jackson with Pepsi and Cindy Crawford's association with L'Oreal.

Product champions need not necessarily have been celebrities in the first place. Sometimes people become minor celebrities through the endorsement of a particular product or service. In the UK, Bernard Matthews, owner of a huge turkey products company, became famous for appearing in commercials for his company's own products. This helped to give the company a more human face and worked well in contrast to a number of other processed food companies, who were faceless and impersonal in the eyes of many consumers. Recently Halifax building society ran a series of TV commercials featuring various of their employees singing the praises of their company – literally. These singing employees became national celebrities and helped the public to create a feeling of connection with Halifax.

Distribution Channels

Getting the distribution channels right is important in terms of reaching your target audience for a product. There is probably little point in selling shaver foam in a bookstore or shoes in a deli! Aside from the practical issues associated with reaching an audience, the channels through which the product is distributed are also likely to have an effect on how people perceive it. For example, if you are trying to create an image as a luxury brand then it is not going to do your image any good if you sell your products through thrift stores.

Similarly if you are manufacturing a value-for-money brand then it may not be wise to sell it in a high-end boutique as the product is likely to look down-market compared to the other items on the shelves. Sometimes finding the correct distribution channel for the product may mean deviating from your normal outlets. For example, when Philips Electronics created a special range of kitchen products in association with Italian design studio Alessi they sold a number of these in specialist design shops and galleries rather than through their usual outlets, the high-street electrical retailers.

Price Point

Stella Artois commercials used to state that their beer was 'reassuringly expensive'. The high cost set a social premium on the beer and gave the drinker a badge of socio-economic status. We are left in little doubt about the socio-economic class of Vertu phone owners. You can't be doing too badly if you can hand over $20 000 for a phone! Setting the price of products is notoriously difficult. You can work it out as a margin on costs, but sometimes it's best just to charge what you think the product's worth. One client of mine in the consumer electronics makes a return of three times cost on one of their products, a margin several orders of magnitude bigger than the industry norm. Their attitude is simply, 'It doesn't matter how much it cost to make, that's what it's worth.' Consumers agree. It's a huge hit in the marketplace. Sometimes a high price is what gives stuff credibility. When

Turtle Wax first came on the market it sold for one dollar a can. But who's going to wax their brand new car with a one-dollar-a-can wax? Not many people, it turned out. They put the price up to five dollars without making any changes to the product and it sold like hot cakes! The price had given it credibility. 'Pricing up' can help give a product prestige and credibility, but there are profits to be made at the budget end of the market too. 'Stack 'em high and sell 'em low' has long worked for Wal-Mart and other superstores, and manufacturers who can supply and sell volume can still succeed even with low margins.

Case Study Part 3 – Delivering Product Benefits

We have looked at elements that we can use in order to build a great experience with a product. Now let's go back to the example of our photo camera for young, high-socio-economic status women and see how we could use various of these elements in order to design and market a camera that our target group will really love. First, let's take a check on the product benefits that we're looking to deliver. Then we'll look at them one by one with suggestions about how they could be delivered. Again, we will keep our persona, Leigh, at the center of our thoughts, although once in a while we may have to cut a little slack to make sure we don't exclude others who might want to use it.

PRODUCT BENEFITS

Camera should feel good in the hand.

Camera should be easy to carry around.

Camera should fit well and comfortably against the face.

Camera should be operable without causing damage to the user's fingernails.

Camera should confer the impression of high socio-economic status on the user.

Camera should confer the impression of high cultural status on the user.

Camera should enable the user to take photos quickly.

Camera should be operable without disturbing others or embarrassing user.

Camera should enable the user to take good quality photos.

Camera should be easy to use at the first attempt.

Camera should look great.

Camera should reflect the user's femininity.

Camera should be environmentally 'safe'.

Camera Should Feel Good in the Hand

The key elements here are the form and the materials. The product should be the right size and shape so that it fits comfortably into Leigh's hand. Although we might be designing it primarily for women, it's a fair bet that men will want to use it too. Certainly we would hope we could also sell the product to men. The product should be designed so that it fits a range of adult hands — from small women to large men. The form and the materials are both likely to affect how it feels in the hand. It will feel good if the product sits nicely in the hand, the weight is well-distributed and the material feels good to the touch.

Camera Should be Easy to Carry Around

Again the form and material will play a major role here. If it's going to be carried in the hand or a bag we want something that is not too heavy and not too big. We need to be a little careful on the weight issue. If it's too light it may be perceived as lacking in quality.

Fits Well and Comfortably Against the Face

It is important that the camera is shaped so as not to jab into the face when being used. The materials used in the camera should also feel comfortable against the face.

Camera Should be Operable Without Causing Damage to the User's Fingernails

Small buttons and catches, which Leigh may use her fingernails to operate, should be designed so that they do not offer a level of resistance that is likely to cause long fingernails to get broken. Alternatively, the design should avoid buttons and catches that will require fingernail operation. It is, then, the properties of the interaction design that are likely to be important here.

Camera Should Confer the Impression of High Socio-economic Status on the User

Make sure the camera looks expensive. Go for classy materials, such as metals and silicones ahead of plastics. Make sure it oozes quality. Better to be thin and heavy rather than bulky or too light. Make sure that the marketing campaign shows the products as the sort of thing that a young, successful woman would have. If you've picking a slot for a TV commercial put it on when Leigh would be watching. Sell the camera in up-scale outlets. Selfridges and Sharper Edge, for example.

Camera Should Confer the Impression of High Cultural Status on the User

The aesthetic elements are the ones that play the biggest role here. Make sure that it is expensive and tasteful rather than expensive and vulgar. Get someone sophisticated to endorse the product. Kate Moss would be great if you could afford her fees!

Camera Should Enable the User to Take Photos Quickly

Make it a point-and-shoot. Automate everything – auto-focus, auto-iris, auto-flash, auto-wind and auto-just-about-everything-else! Put an easy-on-easy-off lens cover on it such as a slide back so she doesn't have to mess around trying to get the lens cap on and off every time she wants to take a photo.

Camera Should be Operable Without Disturbing Others or Embarrassing User

Make sure that all the moving parts are quiet in operation. The last thing Leigh wants is motors whirring away full blast when she's in a gallery or a museum. Some functions, such as rewinding the film, can take some time to complete. If the motor makes too much noise or a dumb-sounding noise it can be really embarrassing, especially if the product is supposed to be sophisticated.

Camera Should Enable the User to Take Good Quality Photos

This shouldn't be too much of a problem. Even fairly low-end cameras take pretty good photos these days. There's no need to bust the development budget trying to come up with new technology to make a better quality of photograph. If Leigh were a professional photographer it might be a different story, but all she is after is good album-quality snaps.

Camera Should be Easy to Use at the First Attempt

The automatic features should be a great help here. Make sure the buttons are placed so that everything is pretty obvious and label them using clear icons. Don't do anything weird with the interaction design and if she's going to need to use the manual at all make sure there's a summary overview in the front.

Camera Should Look Great
Materials, form, color, and graphics are all very important here. Make sure the packaging looks great too, so that it has a chance of catching her eye on the shelf. There are no fixed rules as to what 'good looking' is, but make sure that it fits well with the aesthetic trends of the day.

Camera Should Reflect the User's Femininity
The aesthetic elements are important here again. Don't make it look patronizing, but don't make it a boring black box either. If going for celebrity endorsement choose a product champion who fits with her values. Someone smart, strong, attractive and successful. Venus Williams? Halle Berry? Madonna?

Camera Should Be Environmentally Safe
Materials again! Also make sure the manufacturing processes are efficient. The packaging and manual could use recycled materials.

5
Getting it right

The Three Steps

Making great stuff that people love involves doing three key things:

1. Understanding the people who you are making the stuff for.
2. Working out what they want from the stuff you are making for them.
3. Making and promoting the stuff in such a way that it delivers those things that they want.

Design for the Persona

Put like that it all sounds pretty simple. In some ways it is. Certainly the concept is simple. You might think it is pretty much a no-brainer. However, in my own career I have seen companies and products fail, not because they didn't carry out the three steps above well, but because they didn't even carry them out at all. Some companies have no idea who their target audience is. Some say it is 'everyone'. They might as well say, 'no one'. They embark on a creation process with no idea at all as to who they are designing for. In the end, of course, everyone ends up using a different point of reference as to what the customer might want. Often this ends up being themselves. When members of a development team start talking in terms such as 'I'd never have this in my home', 'I think yellow looks great' or 'I can't imagine my husband ever using it', then the alarm bells should start to ring. Usually the best answer to any of these questions is, 'Who cares? We're not designing the product for you or your spouse.' (Unless of course you are designing the product for these people and their spouses, in which case listen good!)

The power of the persona is that they are an embodiment of the target audience for whom the product is being developed. Personas make a great point of reference in the creation process and they keep everyone properly focussed. In the companies with the best product-creation processes, people come to think of the various personas they use as being like familiar, but demanding, friends. I encourage my clients to think like that. When people start saying things like 'Leigh would love this, I can just imagine it in her living room next to that new stereo she bought' or 'I can't imagine Dave using that, not with his bad hip' then you can bet we are getting someplace. We are no longer designing for an abstract undefined customer, but rather we are all designing for a particular person, albeit a fictitious one. We are all pulling in the same direction and all bending over backwards to satisfy the demands of Leigh, Dave or whoever else our persona happens to be.

Think Big

Working out what people want from the product or service that you are developing is so much richer when a framework such as the four pleasures is applied. That's because the four pleasures help us to look into every area of people's lives and consider what role, if any, the product might play. Too many companies take an impoverished approach to defining the benefits that a product should bring to its user. They don't take the big view. 'It's a camera, so it should allow the user to take photos.' True, but that's not all it is. It's a fashion accessory, a social badge, an ideological statement, a sensorial experience or more or less than this, depending on who the user is. It's vital that a product performs its primary function to an acceptable level of quality, but it's got to do so much more. Some products fail because while they may connect with the head, they don't make it with the heart. This problem often seems to occur when companies take cost-benefit approaches to approaching their market.

Pitfall 1: Cost-benefit Approaches

Cost-benefit theories are formal ways of saying that what people want is the 'biggest bang for their buck'. In other words, give people the best performance or the most features for the lowest possible price and they'll love you for it and buy your product. This approach is usually far too narrow in two senses. On the one hand it reflects a narrow view of the role that the product plays in people's lives. On the other it tends to put far more emphasis on the measurable aspects of a product at the expense of some of the intangibles, in particular aesthetics, which can contribute so much to people's enjoyment of a product.

Cost-benefit approaches to the market can also be pretty weak from a business viewpoint. The problem is that making them work tends to commit a company to a low retail price for the product. You have to cut margins and reduce costs to keep up with your competitors. You are extremely vulnerable to issues outside of your control, such as currency price fluctuations. In short, you are in a commodity market and, as the king of the stock market Warren Buffet once said, 'Never invest in commodities!' The process described in this book is a value-add process. It is based on the premise that if you really understand the users' needs and meet those needs, then people will be willing to pay a fair price for your product or service.

Pitfall 2: Art Design

The ugly sister of the cost-benefit approach to marketing is the 'art-design' approach. This approach is based on the idea that it doesn't much matter what the product does as long as it looks great. The problem with such approaches is that often the consumer gets so ticked off trying to use the product that their attitudes towards the product as a whole are soured regardless of how great it looks. A modern-day classic example of this is the over-animated website. Consumers enter to try to find information about a product they want to buy or a service they want to use, but before they can get the information they need, they have to sit through a long animated sequence. Titles whiz backwards and forwards across the screen, graphics flash, tunes jingle. The user has to sit there watching all this before they can get the information they need. The screens look beautiful, but the chances are that the user is getting more and more irritated the longer it goes on.

The problem with art-design approaches is that they can be self-indulgent. It's fun to do this stuff and it impresses our colleagues! The problem is that it probably doesn't impress our potential customers! Whenever people in design or marketing teams talking about 'educating the customers' that's when the alarm bells should start ringing on the self-indulgence detector. These approaches aren't about working out what the user wants. They have more to do the design and marketing team expressing themselves! Of course art-design approaches aren't just limited to the design of websites. We see products that might look OK but are difficult to use, commercials that are interesting to look at but where we don't remember what was being advertised, or that get some sort of point across but don't help to sell the product.

It is important to distinguish between self-indulgent approaches to design and the use of artistic expression to create a niche-market product that will be a genuine joy for people to own . . . if not always use. Some of the stuff that comes out of the Alessi studio in Milan looks weird and unconventional and it's not always easy to use. Nevertheless, it works because it is designed with people who love humorous, unconventional design in mind. In this sense, the design is user-centered. The designers are sharing their ideas and humor with people who will appreciate it and who want to engage on that level. It's never going to be mass-market stuff, but it can create a lucrative niche opportunity.

Pitfall 3: Commercial Darwinism

A third often tried and rarely successful approach to creating products and services is 'commercial Darwinism'. The idea here is that you get a new idea and throw it out on the market before anyone else gets around to doing it. The big question here is whether you're going to open up a whole new market, or whether you're going to find out that there is no market at all for your idea. Sadly, it is usually the latter. This approach is about survival of the fittest. Given that the idea here is to throw products and services onto the market because they're clever rather than because they're useful, the chances are that only a very few will work out. If you're one of the lucky ones this approach could make you very rich. But then again so could playing the lottery!

Pitfall 4: Fragmentation of the Decision Process

Having understood the users and what they want, one of the keys to making stuff that they love is to understand the elements of a design and marketing campaign that can be used to deliver this. These things are our building blocks. We can use them to build the user experience. We have to combine them in such a way that they complement each other in getting the right message across. A common mistake is to lose sight of how a particular element may affect people's experience of the product. For example, you can make an elegant, sophisticated-looking product, but if it feels cheap to the touch, then the elegance factor is going to diminish pretty quickly in the eyes of your customers. Similarly, you might run a great campaign on TV showing how seriously your company takes its environmental responsibilities and then discover that your company has sponsored an off-road race through an area of great natural beauty, much to the chagrin of environmentalists. Mistakes like these tend to occur when a company is highly decentralized in its management and functional structure. In highly decentralized organizations it is not always clear where responsibilities lie. This can lead to disjointed decision-making in the creation process.

This is not to say that decentralization is all bad. For example, the people in the China office are likely to be better informed as to what will work in the markets there than the people back in New York or wherever the headquarters happen to be. The danger, though, is of an employee acting like a 'loose cannon' – making a decision about one of the design and marketing elements on their own, with the possibility that this steps out of line with the overall experience that we are trying to get across. A Central-Europe-based client of mine, for example, was horrified when they saw the series of print commercials that their UK office had sanctioned in a number of lifestyle magazines. The aim throughout the product creation process had been to design and promote a product that was sophisticated, stylish and environmentally responsible. Something just right for the modern man. Unfortunately, the print ads that were placed in the magazines were written in a style that was aimed at a quite different audience. The prose was the kind that was more likely to appeal to a redneck than a new man. Considering that the magazines were in part aimed at a tasteful, up-scale readership – in other words the new man himself – the mistake was even worse. These guys were going to see the company making a complete dumb-ass out of itself and ruin the image of the product into the bargain.

This sort of thing is all too common. A common example of this in the design process is the separation of decisions about the aesthetic elements of a product, such as form, color and materials, from each other. In particular, product colors are often selected after the rest of the design is complete and often by a different group of people from those involved in the other aesthetic elements of the design. Of course, an even more common type of separation that occurs is that between the design process and the marketing campaign. In nearly all companies, design and marketing are perceived as being separate functions. This is understandable. They are, after all, different disciplines that require different skill sets. The danger comes when they don't talk to each other often enough. In many companies the two hardly have any contact with each other. Designers design stuff and pass it on to engineers who make it. Then it arrives in the marketing department who try to work out how to sell it.

The problem is that although the design team and the marketing team are doing their best to create a great experience for the consumer, their efforts may not be complementary. If they haven't explicitly agreed what the key product benefits are and how to reach consumers, then there is a danger that there may be an inconsistency between the message that comes across in the design of the product and the marketing message. The marketing team may decide that in order to persuade the target group to buy the product they need to put together a campaign with an emphasis on one set of qualities. The design team may have felt that there were other qualities that were more important to the users. Of course they have created the design with these qualities in mind. This leads to an incongruence between what design team has created and what the marketing team are selling – a very common situation in many industries. The key here is to bring all those involved in creating the experience of the product together at the start of the process. Designers and marketers should have a common understanding of what benefits the product or service is delivering and how these benefits should be delivered in both the design and marketing campaign. All the relevant elements should be brought together in order to create a coherent and consistent set of benefits for consumers.

Research the Persona

This book outlines a process for creating great stuff that people will love. But we have to remember that it is just a process. Going through the three stages is vital, but of course it isn't enough in and of itself. It's not only a matter of doing it, it's also a matter of doing it well. When creating a persona to represent the consumer in the design process the accuracy of this persona, in terms of being a representative member of the target group, is going to depend on how much you know about the target group. If you've got a bunch of market research data about the characteristics then build the persona based on that. It's probably going to be better than having to work purely on the basis of professional judgement. Nevertheless, sensible professional judgement is going to be better than just basing a persona on your mom, or your dad or your sister.

Check Your Assumptions

Similarly, when you are looking into the kinds of benefits that people want from products and services, you're probably going get a better picture if you go out and ask a few of them. If you've got the market research budget available, evaluate some of the decisions that you have made. Maybe some of the things I assumed about Leigh's tastes and preferences when working through the camera example were wrong. If I had the budget I'd want to commission some market research institute to go out and test some of those assumptions.

Make Professional Judgements

Once you're clear about the benefits that you want to deliver, you need to decide how to deliver them and how to execute that delivery. This is something that comes down to the skill and judgement of the designers, marketers and others in the product development team. For example, do you get across socio-economic status mainly through the materials used for the product, the functionality of the product, the way it's packaged, the TV commercials? All of these? None of these? Just a couple of them? This really is a judgement call. You can do some research and see what worked and what didn't work before, but in the end someone's got to make a call. The same with how you execute stuff. You may have decided you want the model on the packaging to look like a new man, but what does a new man look like? Or to put it another way, what do new men aspire to look like? In the end professional skill and expertise will have to be brought to bear on these things. The better the people you've got working on that project, the better you are at your own job, the greater the chance of making great stuff.

Skill and Tactics

No process can make a great product by itself. If you want great products you need great professionals to make them and market them. Think of it like sport. You're never going to win the Super Bowl without great players, but you've also got to have great tactics to win the Super Bowl. Processes such as the one outlined in this book are to product and service creation and promotion as tactics are to sport. The problem that many companies face is that they get their tactics wrong. An overwhelming majority of new product launches still fail. So do the vast majority of new businesses. These failures are very rarely through lack of talent. There are some great people out there, and design and marketing schools are turning out more great grads every year.

Not getting the tactics right is by far the most common cause of failure. Either not having any tactics at all or having the kind of tactics, such as some of those we looked at above, that just don't cut it in today's marketplace. Compared with other approaches, the success rate for products developed using the process outlined here is extremely impressive. The approach is so successful because it is both simple and thorough. I've got a lot of rich clients out there and they've each got a whole bunch of very satisfied customers. This approach gets the whole team playing together, working determinedly for customers and meeting every challenge to ensure delivery of the very highest quality. The approach personalizes the customer and makes explicit the importance of every last detail of the design and marketing of the product. It is a process that creates pride and passion in the design and marketing teams. We've got that customer in our minds and we're sure as heck going to make sure that they are going to love what we are making for them.

Go for It!

What we've got in this little book is a great approach to creating products and services that people will love. The approach is great because it's holistic and integrated. It looks at people in their entirety and at products and services in their entirety. It is simple. There are only three steps, but it is extremely thorough. It requires that we get to know our customers in great detail and to make a real commitment to understanding them and addressing their needs, wants and desires in the products and services that we create for them. It also requires us to get to grips with all of the elements of design and marketing and to ensure that we address all of these in our quest to please the customer. This approach is about achieving commercial success through an attention to detail, a respect for the consumer and a full-on commitment to pleasing them. These are the keys to making great stuff that people love and making big money out of it.

BIBLIOGRAPHY

Lewis, C.S., *The Four Loves*, Harcourt Brace International, 1971
Tiger, Lionel, *The Pursuit of Pleasure*, Little, Brown, 1992